IMMORTAL LOVE

SAINTLY DEVOTEES OF GURUVAYUR

IMMORTAL LOVE

SAINTLY DEVOTEES OF GURUVAYUR

SULINI V. NAIR

Indus Source Books
42/43C, Balaji Bhavan,
Sakal Bhavan Road, Sector 11,
CBD Belapur, Navi Mumbai 400614
INDIA
Email: info@indussource.com
www.indussource.com

Immortal Love: Saintly Devotees of Guruvayur

ISBN: 978-93-85509-75-9

Cover and inside illustrations by Sajeev Sebastian

Cover design by Sonal Churi, Mumbai

Printed at Shefali Arts, Mumbai

For my parents,
Who look upon every sick person
that comes to them as a living embodiment
of Guruvayurappan.

Main entrance to the Guruvayur Temple

CONTENTS

Temple pond

FOREWORD

In many ways, this book does something extraordinary since it tells the stories of five devotees whose lives revolve around the same central theme. The common factor is that all of them – four men and one woman – are known for their extraordinary devotion to one particular deity in one particular temple. As such the potential reader might expect their stories to be somewhat similar and then wonder why, since the book focuses on Lord Krishna, a deity known and worshipped throughout India, the different regions, temples, and aspects of Krishna weren't selected. Yet Sulini Nair knows why, as does every devotee who comes before the presiding deity of Kerala's Guruvayur Temple: Lord Krishna, locally known as Guruvayurappan, the Lord of Guruvayur Temple.

Her deep respect and knowledge gently peels back the centuries to tell us about the five individuals, telling their stories in a way that allows the reader to not only understand how deeply Guruvayurappan is revered but also how deeply these devotees are still regarded, centuries after their deaths.

Each short chapter lays out the life of a particular devotee, allowing the reader to see and understand their particular story. The five: Poothanam Nambootiri, Melputhur Narayana Bhattathiri, Manavedan Raja, Vilwamangalam Swamiyar, and the one woman, Kururamma are deftly sketched and brought to life, revealing their failings, pains and, ultimately — and always — their deep faith.

It is this aspect of the book, the uniting of the remarkable devotees, that we come to realise how extraordinary it is that, despite their differences and stories, they are all unknowingly 'united' by the divine persona of an extraordinary deity, one depicted and worshipped as a small boy.

***Padma Shri* Pepita Seth**
Author and Photographer

INTRODUCTION

One of the facets of India's spiritual tradition is the apotheosis of devotion as a hallmark of divinity. The story of mortals becoming immortal through the choicest and most self-effacing effort has glorified the story of many a mahatma and *mahima sthali* across the length and breadth of the country.

A few centuries ago, in the idyllic shrine of Sri Krishna at Guruvayur in Kerala too, such stories of aspiration and devotion played out to reverberate through time. The entrancing glory of Sri Krishna at Guruvayur became part of the lore, lyric, literature, and life of generations through the lives of a handful of saintly devotees.

The Guruvayur Sri Krishna temple in the Thrissur district of Kerala is one of the holiest shrines in this region. Thronged by millions of devotees, Sri Krishna is worshipped here as a naughty little child.

A Sanskrit work named *Guruvayu-pura-mahatmyam* supposed to embody a dialogue between Sage Atreya and King Janamejaya, is the source of the temple's *sthala purana* or traditional account of origin. Though much of it might be legendary, it is significant from a devotional viewpoint.

The idol is not said to be of earthly origin. Made of a material called the "*patalasila*", Sri Mahavishnu is said to have given it to Brahma who gave it to a rishi named Sutapas. He gave it to Kasyapa-Prajapati who gave it to Vasudeva, Sri Krishna's father. Sri Krishna installed and worshipped it at Dwarka, His capital. Before His ascent to heaven, Sri Krishna told His devotee and minister Uddhava that the idol would come floating after Dwarka was engulfed by the ocean. He was asked to communicate this to *Brihaspati,* the Guru of devas, and request him to install it in a suitable place for the spiritual uplift of mankind in the *Kali Yuga.*

Accordingly, the idol was taken by *Brihaspati,* and along with *Vayu* (the Wind God), he went all over the world looking for a sacred spot to install it. As directed by Lord Shiva, they installed it at a place in the coastal region of Kerala near Ambapura. Since it was installed by Guru and *Vayu,* the place came to be called "Guruvayur". According to this legendary history, the temple must be considered more than 5,100 years old, if it had been consecrated soon after Sri Krishna's *swargarohana.* As the idol is said to have had its origin in *Vaikuntha*, devotees began to look upon the temple as *Bhuloka Vaikuntha* or earthly *Vaikuntha.*

King Janamejaya, the grandson of the Pandavas destroyed serpents in his *sarpa-satra* or snake sacrifice to avenge the death of his father Parikshit by the serpent Takshaka's bite. The serpents' curse led him to be afflicted with leprosy. Sage Atreya advised him to offer worship at Guruvayur temple and he was cured only after long years of worshipping Sri Krishna there.

The full-fledged temple came into existence at an unknown

date. The story goes that an astrologer predicted that a Pandya king would be bitten by a snake in ten months. The king spent this time visiting holy places which included Guruvayur. At the end of ten months, he returned home without mishap and took the astrologer to task for his false prediction. The astrologer told the king that he would have the mark of a snake bite on his left leg and that he had escaped death only by his being at a temple where Anantha, the king of serpents, was present and because the king had resolved to rebuild that holy shrine. That holy shrine was Guruvayur. Convinced by the astrologer's words, he built a beautiful temple for Sri Krishna at Guruvayur.

In some time, the temple was reduced to poverty for lack of patronage from the Shaivite Perumal kings. The nearby Shiva temple at Mammiyur received their patronage and devotees started to throng there.

One day, a holy man went to the Shiva temple for food and hospitality for the night. Though they could very well have looked after him, they pretended to have nothing and contemptuously directed him to the Guruvayur temple knowing only too well the condition there. When the man went to Guruvayur, he was received courteously and fed well by a brahmin boy. The pleased man spoke a blessing — as the authorities at Mammiyur had said, "The Guruvayur temple would enjoy abundance thereafter while there would be nothing at Mammiyur." It is said that from that day, that was exactly what happened.

Looking at the origin of the temple from a historical viewpoint, the actual temple records date only from the seventeenth century. The present sanctum dates from only AD 1638. By this time, the temple was already very prominent. Therefore, we cannot say anything about the antiquity of the temple from actual records and references. The songs of the Alwars, whose time was up to the eighth century, have the earliest mention of the significant Vishnu temples of Kerala. But we find no mention of Guruvayur temple in those. This temple is also not mentioned in the many extant copper plates and stone engravings giving the list of important temples of Kerala up to the twelfth century. A fifteenth century poetic work *Kokasandesa* refers to a place "Kuruvayur" in the region where the temple now exists. So, all that we could say with certainty is that between the twelfth and the seventeenth centuries, a Sri Krishna temple grew in prominence at a place formerly called "Kuruvayur", now Guruvayur, thanks to the Guru and *Vayu* connection.

By the beginning of the eighteenth century, its prominence attracted the predatory attention of the Dutch (1716) and Tipu Sultan (1789) who attacked, plundered, and burnt parts of the temple. The idol was saved by the priests by shifting it to the Sri Krishna temple at Ambalappuzha in the erstwhile Travancore region during Tipu's attack, and brought back later. Afterwards, the temple progressed steadily. Originally managed by the Zamorin kings, it is now governed by the Guruvayur Devaswom, a statutory body.

This originally unknown temple was brought into great prominence by five great, saintly devotees. Their lives and experiences began to evoke faith and devotion in increasing numbers of people. These five devotees lived between the middle of the sixteenth and the end of the seventeenth centuries. Especially since then, little Krishna of Guruvayur has been the divine beloved of millions of devotees. These devotees continue to live in the collective consciousness of Keralites. Miraculous stories associated with them are still part of the temple legends and devotional folklore of Kerala.

All of them, except for Kururamma, the lone woman devotee, have composed exquisite works in Sanskrit and Malayalam.

This book presents the life and experiences of these five great devotees of Sri Krishna namely, Poonthanam Nambootiri, Melputhur Narayana Bhattathiri, Manavedan Raja, Vilwamangalam Swamiyar, and Kururamma. Poonthanam's *Jnanappana,* Melputhur's *Narayaneeyam,* and Vilwamangalam's *Sri Krishna Karnamritam* are, even today, an indispensable part of not only the Guruvayur temple but also of the lives of countless devotees and scholars. Manavedan Raja's seminal contribution is the *Krishnageeti,* to which the *Krishnanattam* is still danced within the Guruvayur temple, every night as an offering.

However, more than these or other literary achievements, these personages stand tall in the hearts of ordinary devotees through the strength and sweetness of their devotion to Guruvayurappan; giving Kururamma also a prominent place among them.

Today, the Guruvayur temple is not merely a famous place of worship thronged by millions of devotees throughout the year; it is verily an emotion. Sri Krishna there is not a mere idol worshipped with reverential devotion; to the devotees, it is verily *Balagopala* Himself, the naughty divine child, who is one's own to love, adore, worship, chastise, and belong to. Stepping into the temple is to step into a constant festival of joy.

It is said that there is no difference between the *Bhagavata, Bhagavan,* and bhakta – the scripture, the Lord, and the devotee are equally to be venerated. Such is the stature of the true devotee. Diving deep into the lives of these great devotees of Guruvayurappan who brought glory to this temple is an opportunity to be sanctified by the blessing of pure devotion.

Just as one becomes affluent merely by fraternising with the wealthy, so does one who associates with Your devotees, gain an abundance of devotion towards You. May I be blessed with such contacts. May I also be blessed with that deep devotion that destroys all sins.

– Narayaneeyam

Chapter 91, Verse 4

Resources

1) Bhattatiri, M.N., Narayaneeyam: Bhagavata Condensed, Translated by Swami Tapasyananda, Chennai: Sri Ramakrishna Math, 1976.
2) Melputhur Narayana Bhattathiri, Narayaneeyam. Translated by Ram Varmha, Published by Mrs Rama Varmha Thampuran, 1978.

Chapter 1

POONTHANAM NAMBOOTIRI (1547–1640)

Sixteenth century Kerala was a society ridden with the evil effects of feudalism and the caste system. Among the Nambootiri brahmins of Kerala, not all were rich landlords. There was also a large group who were poor and worked as priests in temples and conducted ritual pujas and *homas* for a living. Some of them also travelled from place to place conducting readings from the *Srimad Bhagavata*. The devotee-poet Poonthanam was one such brahmin who had neither rank nor wealth, only a cursory education, and struggled hard to survive.

He was born in a Nambootiri family at the Poonthanam *Illam* in what is now the Keezhattur village, eight kilometres north of Perinthalmanna in the Malappuram district of Kerala. Though he came to be known as "Poonthanam Nambootiri", his real name is not known. Right from his childhood he was deeply devoted to his family deity Tirumandhamkunnu Bhagavati and grew up in a life of austerity and surrender.

He often visited the Tirumandhamkunnu temple at Angadippuram. The family also had a shrine in their house where the *Bhagavati* was installed and worshipped daily. Gradually Poonthanam developed an affinity for the Divine in the form of Sri Krishna. He felt drawn to Guruvayur and undertook the arduous trek to Guruvayur through dense forest every month, resting at some benevolent home each night. Sri Krishna's name began to dance forever on his lips and His form in his heart.

Even though he lived each moment savouring the utter sweetness of the divine name, there was one sorrow that gnawed at Poonthanam's heart — that of being childless.

Finally, after many years, he was blessed with a child. The family's joy knew no bounds. Months passed and it was the day of the baby's *annaprashan.* It was a very joyous occasion and the family had invited many guests. The baby was given a bath, dressed, and laid to sleep on the bedroom floor. Womenfolk who arrived from far and near were busy getting ready. After a while, to their horror, they realised that some of them had unwittingly left their clothes in a heap on the hapless baby who suffocated to death.

Poonthanam already knew that everything in this world was transient. But this great tragedy drove home this truth with deep intensity. In the heights of sorrow and dispassion, and struck by the meaninglessness of the joys of this world, he composed the celebrated *Jnanappana* or the Song of Wisdom. In simple language the *Jnanappana* expounds deep Vedantic philosophy, in a manner that nurtures dispassion, relating it to the *prarabdha*-ridden life of ordinary individuals. It sings of the meaninglessness of worldly pursuits, the arrogance of wealth and ancestry, and the beauty and effectiveness of chanting the divine name in *Kali Yuga*. The distraught father transformed his deepest sorrow most extraordinarily into his greatest sadhana and sang,

Poonthanam mourns the loss of his child

Poonthanam feeds Balagopala

...We enter this world all alone
We leave it all alone too.
In this brief interlude when we meet,
How worthless is rivalry!
When life finds richness in the goal of purushartha,
Why yearn for paltry material riches?
The splendour of the noonday sun could be ours...
Why then settle for the meagre firefly!
When baby Krishna dances in our hearts,
Why, ever, do we need babies of our own?

– (Jnanappana)

Sorrow could truly be a great teacher. Parikshit's sorrow born of an agonizing fear of death gifted us the *Srimad Bhagavata,* and Arjuna's deep grief born of genuine angst gave us the *Bhagavad Gita.* In these cases, sorrow was not *roga* but verily yoga, spiritual striving, that led to the expounding of ultimate truths that would redeem all of mankind.

When Poonthanam truly understood that he could not depend on anything external, he experienced complete surrender and deep bhakti which led to the dawn of pure *jnana.* He experienced *Balagopala* within his heart as a constant living presence. Having or not having a human child ceased to matter. He felt fulfilled. He was thus free from desire and sorrow.

Established in a state of inner oneness with Sri Krishna, poetry flowed spontaneously from his heart. It was full of wisdom and for the good of the world. Such poetry composed in a state of oneness with the Divine, is timeless. The rendering of such poetry is soothing and comforting to even those who may not know the language simply because the words have flowed from a pure heart. There may be several poets who compose philosophical works; but when philosophy melts in the crucible of painful life experience, it undergoes a magical transformation and flows into artistic creation with delicate sensitivity. In poetry, the words then swell and tremble with the unmatched richness of wisdom born of experience, and they touch and transform lives.

The humble soul who composed poetry in conversational Malayalam was looked down upon by other Nambootiri scholars who composed in Sanskrit, but his devotion never failed to move even the hardest critics. The miracle of pure bhakti shines through the many wondrous episodes from his seemingly commonplace life, teaching subtly yet unmistakably that to acquire knowledge is all very well, but the path to the Beyond is ultimately a process of un-learning and un-becoming everything that is of this world.

Sanskrit and Vedic scholars of the Kudalloor *Mana* were wealthy and conceited. As they came to know about Poonthanam's unique *Bhagavata* expositions, they invited him to their house to read for them. When Poonthanam began to read the *Bhagavata* and explain the text, the listeners, most moved by his blessed state of supreme devotion, prostrated at his feet, and sought pardon.

Once, Poonthanam was reading the *Karhichidadhyaya* in the tenth canto of the *Bhagavata* at the Kottiyoor Shiva temple in north Kerala; the *Karhichidadhyaya* describes the lovers' quarrel between Sri Krishna and Rukmini. When he finished his reading, he placed a bookmark on the page he had stopped at and closed the book.

When he opened the book to resume reading the next day, he found that the bookmark had been placed at the beginning of the same section that he had read the previous day. When he found the same thing happening day after day, he thought someone was trying to fool him. That night, Lord Shiva appeared in his dream and said to Poonthanam, "I cannot have enough of your reading of that chapter Poonthanam! It was I who moved your bookmark."

When Poonthanam finally finished his reading of the *Bhagavata* at the Kottiyoor temple and was about to leave the place, he went to take his *Bhagavata* book. He found Lord Shiva Himself seated at the place reading the *Karhichidadhyaya*! Devi Sri Parvati sat listening nearby. He overheard Devi say that though *Bhagavan's* reading was good, as far as devotion was concerned, Poonthanam's reading was superior! As this story spread, Poonthanam came to be called *"Karhichid Bhattathiri"*.

One Monday, as was his usual routine, Poonthanam was on his way to the Guruvayur temple for his Monday worship. It was not an easy journey. But Poonthanam walked, enjoying himself chanting the divine name all the way. By late evening when he reached the forest region of Koottanad, he suddenly found himself accosted by four to five hefty robbers. They snatched his money and a gold ring he wore. Fearing they would be caught if they let him go, they decided to kill him. Thinking intensely of *Bhagavan's* feet, Poonthanam prayed,

यात्वराद्रौपदीत्राणे
यात्वरागजरक्षणे
मय्यार्तेकरुणामूर्ते
सात्वराक्वगताहरे!

"The kind of anguish You had to save Draupadi and Gajendra, where did such anguish go in the case of my cries, O Hari!"

Suddenly someone appeared there in the form of the Zamorin king's minister Mangattachan and rescued Poonthanam from the robbers. Overcome with gratitude,

Poonthanam gifted his gold ring to Mangattachan.

That night, the priest at the Guruvayur temple received this instruction in a dream, "The *Pavithra* ring seen on the idol belongs to Poonthanam. Return it to him."

The next morning the priest found the ring on the idol and gave it to Poonthanam along with prasad. Everyone present at the temple that morning for the *Nirmalyadarshan* rejoiced at this and sang Krishna's glory.

One day, Poonthanam was chanting the *Vishnu Sahasranama* at the Guruvayur temple. The great Sanskrit poet and scholar Melputhur Narayana Bhattathiri was at the temple too. He overheard Poonthanam chant "*Padmanabho Maraprabhu*" and corrected him saying, "Padmanabha is *Amaraprabhu*; not *Maraprabhu*!" Just then a voice was heard from within the sanctum sanctorum, "I am *Maraprabhu* and *Amaraprabhu*. I am *Sarvaprabhu*!" Melputhur, the author of the *Narayaneeyam*, was himself a great devotee of Guruvayurappan. It was after composing this work that he was cured of the arthritis that he had taken on from his guru.

Once, Poonthanam very respectfully asked Melputhur how he was to meditate on *Bhagavan*. "Meditate on Him in the form of a buffalo!" Melputhur replied in jest. Poonthanam was a simpleton who believed the words of noble people. He innocently took Melputhur's words as *upadesha* from a guru. He started meditating on *Bhagavan* in the form of a buffalo.

One day, during the *Sheeveli* procession, the priest found that he could not move as *Bhagavan's* idol had got stuck in the doorway. No one could find out how the idol got stuck. Melputhur was sitting in the temple reading the *Narayaneeyam*. When the matter was brought to his attention, he looked towards the idol. And lo! He saw in place of *Bhagavan's* idol, the form of a buffalo! Its horns were stuck in the frame of the door!

Manjulaal

Poonthanam Illam

It was a lesson that even an ignorant devotee who chanted the divine name would be blessed to fruitfully meditate upon *Bhagavan* in any form. Also, that even if a devotee like Melputhur said something in jest, his words would carry the power of manifestation. Wonderstruck at *Bhagavan's* immense love for His devotees, Melputhur instructed them to tilt the idol a little to solve the problem. Sure enough, it helped and they were able to continue with the procession.

On one occasion, Poonthanam took his newly composed work *Sri Krishna Karnamritam* to Melputhur and humbly requested him to read it and make corrections. The story goes that Melputhur suggested that Poonthanam show it to some poet who composed works in Malayalam. "How would you know of *vibhakti*?" he is said to have asked.

Later that evening, Melputhur experienced a worsening of his arthritis that had fully been cured earlier. Writhing in pain he cried out to Guruvayurappan until he dozed off out of weariness. That night he had a dream. *Bhagavan* spoke benignly, "Even I cannot save one who hurts by word or deed. My innocent devotee who has surrendered everything to Me. Poonthanam's bhakti is dearer to Me than your *vibhakti*." Melputhur woke with a start and immediately sent for Poonthanam. He prostrated at his feet and sought forgiveness. Melputhur's pain vanished as miraculously as it had manifested, and he duly read through Poonthanam's work.

A poor, young girl Manjula strung a garland for Guruvayurappan every day. One day, she accompanied her mother somewhere far away and was late to reach the temple. She rushed there only to find it closed. Seeing her in tears, Poonthanam gently advised her to offer the garland at the peepal tree at the far end of the eastern entrance. Manjula did so, fervently praying that Sri Krishna should accept her garland. The next morning the priest found that he was unable to remove one of the previous day's garlands from the idol no matter how hard he tried. He finally came out of the sanctum to seek advice. Poonthanam told him that it was Manjula's garland and that it would come off if he tried with reverence. And, so it did. The peepal tree that stands at this spot has been commemorated as the *Manjulaal* (*Aal* is peepal in Malayalam).

Equally renowned as the *Jnanappana* is Poonthanam's *Santhanagopalam Pana*. It is based on the story from the tenth canto of the *Bhagavata*. A poor brahmin whose children had all died seeks Arjuna's help in protecting his unborn child. When Arjuna fails to do so and the child dies, Sri Krishna leads a distraught Arjuna to *Vaikuntha* to reclaim the dead children. At this point, Poonthanam could not compose further because he did not know how to describe *Vaikuntha*! He went to bed feeling lost and deeply troubled.

That night he had a dream. He saw himself travelling somewhere in a beautiful flying carriage. It finally touched ground at *Vaikuntha*. He was welcomed by two divine beings. They showed him around *Vaikuntha* and he took in the stunning sights of palaces, towers, beautiful gardens, and dazzling jewel-studded buildings. *Vaikuntha* was populated by the purest of souls who went about their tasks chanting *Hari nama*. Even bees chanted the hallowed name of *Hari!*

Finally, the beings led Poonthanam to a hall where sages and devotees waited to listen to his exposition of the *Bhagavata*. Poonthanam read from the text. Everyone listened in reverential silence and praised and blessed him. Poonthanam then expressed his heart's desire to have a darshan of *Bhagavan* Mahavishnu. The two beings led him to the divine presence and Poonthanam drank in the divine vision of *Bhagavan* Vishnu reclining on Anantha. Finally, he reluctantly decided to take leave.

At this time the two divine beings fell at Poonthanam's feet saying, "*Sadguro*, be pleased to bless us!" Poonthanam was thoroughly baffled as to how he could be their guru. They explained that in their previous lifetime, they were two jackfruit trees that stood in Poonthanam's courtyard. They were rendered blessed by his daily *Bhagavata* reading and chanting of the divine names. Astounded and overwhelmed, he gently touched the divine beings by way of blessing and got into the flying carriage.

The next morning Poonthanam woke a little later than usual. He was astonished to find that a couple of jackfruit trees that stood in his courtyard had fallen in the previous night's gale. He also found that the bookmark in his copy of the *Bhagavata* had been moved to the page that described *Vaikuntha*. Overjoyed, he composed the *Vaikuntha darshan* in his *Santhanagopalam Pana* based on his dream vision of *Vaikuntha*. Other than these works, Poonthanam composed many more popular hymns and songs in praise of the Divine.

By the time Poonthanam was past ninety-two years of age, he was unable to travel to Guruvayur. Deeply distraught, he prayed intensely at the sanctum of *Bhagavan* Mahavishnu at his ancestral temple.

One day, at a spot to the left of the sanctum, he was blessed with the *darshan* of Sri Krishna as *Balagopala* holding butter in his palm. In a dream, *Bhagavan* said, "I am very pleased with the way you have worshipped Me all your life. You are old now. So, you need not come to Guruvayur to see Me. It is more than enough if you worship Me at home; for wherever My devotee- sings My name I am present."

In the *Padma Purana (Uttara Khanda 92.21), Bhagavan* tells Narada Maharishi,

नाहंवसामिवैकुण्ठेयोगिनांहृदयेनच ।
मद्भक्तात्रगायन्तितत्रतिष्ठामिनारद! ।।

"I dwell not in Vaikuntha, nor in the hearts of yogis; wherever My devotees sing My name, there do I dwell O Narada!"

Poonthanam got a small sub-shrine for Sri Krishna built at the spot at which he had *Bhagavan's* darshan. He then spent nearly all his time in the temple chanting the divine name. His family, and even his wife, dismissed his actions as a mere show. But an unperturbed Poonthanam continued to revel in the bliss of inner communion with the Divine.

Then one night, he again had a dream. Sri Krishna appeared in the dream and told him that He would arrive at Poonthanam's house to partake of his birthday feast. Poonthanam joyfully conveyed this happy news to his family but they simply laughed it off.

On his birthday, at dawn, Poonthanam decorated the house and courtyard as best as he could. He lit lamps and incense and waited with bated breath and tear-filled eyes for Sri Krishna to arrive. The feast was ready. Now and then Poonthanam ran to the foyer to see if Sri Krishna was coming. His family concluded that Poonthanam had gone completely insane.

Finally, Poonthanam heard the notes of the flute and the tinkle of anklets. Little Krishna's charming form appeared wearing a yellow loin cloth and holding His flute! A peacock feather adorned His hair. His little body — of the colour of purple rainclouds — was adorned with sparkling jewels. A beatific smile played upon His lips.

The great devotee finally had the darshan of his *Bhagavan* in the very form in which he had worshipped Him all his life!

Statue of Poonthanam inside the Guruvayur temple

Tears of bliss flowed from Poonthanam's eyes. Chanting the divine name, he welcomed Krishna home.

His family watched stupefied as Poonthanam washed Krishna's feet and offered flowers. He then turned to his family and beseeched them to prostrate before *Bhagavan*. But they saw no *Bhagavan*; just an old man who they thought had gone mad. He prayed to Krishna to reveal Himself to the others. *Bhagavan* smiled and said, "I am helpless. How can those who have no faith in the words of my devotee ever see Me?"

Krishna partook of the feast filling Poonthanam's heart with untold joy. The indifferent attitude of his family broke his heart at the same time. He prayed to Krishna to somehow make them aware of His divine presence. The family members then saw the sweet pudding Poonthanam served *Bhagavan* on the banana leaf disappear miraculously. However, nothing convinced them.

Little Krishna then told Poonthanam that He had come to take him to *Vaikuntha,* and that He was willing to take along anyone who believed in Poonthanam's words. The poet immediately turned towards his family and asked them thrice if anyone wanted to accompany them. His words were met with scorn. The humble maid who stood in the courtyard watching all of this cried, "Master, I want to come! Please take me along!"

Little Krishna took Poonthanam's hand and started to walk. The maid followed. Everyone saw Poonthanam followed by the maid walk to the gate of the courtyard. Suddenly the maid exclaimed, "Here! My master is climbing into *Bhagavan's* carriage! I am going too!" and fell dead.

Poonthanam was never seen or heard of again.

These miraculous stories from Poonthanam's life have endured through the centuries with no overt efforts to ensure the same. Poonthanam continues to live in the collective consciousness of millions of devotees who throng the Guruvayur temple to this day. He has been immortalised by his statue at the outer circumambulatory path of the shrine and by his *Jnanappana* sung in the early hours of the morning every day within the temple. Poonthanam Day is observed in honour of the poet during the Malayalam month of *Kumbham* (mid-February to mid-March) at the Guruvayur temple.

The Poonthanam *Illam* still stands, taken over and managed by the Guruvayur Devaswom, a well-worn building tucked away amidst wild green, resounding with the chirping of birds; an oasis of heritage and history. A priest continues to offer daily worship to the Thirumandhamkunnu Bhagavati in the family shrine room as was the practice since the days of yore. Poonthanam's ancestral temple, now called the "Poonthanam Sri Mahavishnu-Krishna Temple" is the only temple to Mahavishnu with Krishna as an *upadevata.*

The legacy of the great poet is eternal; for through him *Bhagavan* once again revealed that He cares little for scholarship or pedantry but would be attained by the simple, pure-hearted devotee that loves Him.

Resources

1) Achuthamenon, T., *Poonthana Sarvaswom,* Guruvayur: Guruvayur Devaswom, 2010, 461 pp.
2) Aravindakshan, A., *Poonthanam,* New Delhi: Sahitya Akademi, 2014.
3) Aravindan (ed.), *Poonthanam Krithikal,* Kottayam: DC Books, 2008, 258 pp.
4) Bhaktashiromani Poonthanam Nambootiri, *Aanjam Madhavan,* Palakkad: Narayanalayam.
5) Seth, Pepita, *Heaven on Earth: The Universe of Kerala's Guruvayur Temple,* New Delhi: Niyogi Books, 2009.
6) Soman, P., *Poonthanam: Paathavum Pathanavum,* Thiruvananthapuram: The State Institute of Languages, 2011.

Chapter 2

MELPUTHUR NARAYANA BHATTATHIRI (1560–1646)

The drive along the highway from the famous Thirunavaya temple towards Puthanathani in the Ponnani *taluk* and Kurumbathur region of Malappuram district is quite picturesque. About two miles away from Thirunavaya is a nondescript sign on the side of the highway announcing the close by location of Chandanakkavu temple.

It is a quiet wooded grove with a variety of large trees including sandalwood; easy to drive across as just another beautiful countryside vista. But quietly nestled here, not known to many, are the legendary Chandanakkavu temple and the place where once stood the renowned Melputhur *Illam*.

Vasudevan Nambootiri in his poetic work *Bhramarasandesham* describes Chandanakkavu as "the place resonant with the voices of Matrudatta's disciples engaged in learning the shastras". Matrudattan Nambootiri was an authority on the Veda, Mimamsa, Tantra, and other shastras. He married a girl from the Payyur *Illam* which was the ancestral home of scholars well-versed in Mimamsa philosophy. Melputhur Narayana Bhattathiri was their second son.

More than four hundred years ago, the Chandanakkavu temple was a great centre of learning. There are three main temples here; one the *Bhagavati* on the northern side, two Vishnu on the southern side, and Ganapati in the centre. Within each of these, there are many more deities enshrined, and in all, there are eighteen of them. The Ganapati temple was the most prominent and it was here that *Vedadhyayana* took place.

Children from nearby *Illams* congregated at the temple for their lessons under Madhavan Bhattathiri who taught Vedic chanting. Other gurus taught Sanskrit and the Vedas. Matrudattan Nambootiri too taught at the Chandanakkavu temple. He had disciples learning *Vedangas* such as *Shiksha, Chhandas, Vyakarana* and *Nirukta, Mimamsa, Vedanta,* and various Sutras under him.

Young Narayanan, who later came to be known by the name Melputhur, had an elder brother Damodaran, and a younger brother Matrudattan. An astute learner even from early childhood, he must have completed his early education and *upanayanam* followed by basic Sanskrit and Vedic chanting by around the age of twelve. He too learnt under Madhavan Bhattathiri. As soon as he completed his *Vedadhyayana*, he started learning Mimamsa, *Vedanta, Sankhya,* Yoga, and other shastras under his father and *Tarka* under his elder brother Damodaran. While still a student he also started to compose beautiful poetry in Sanskrit.

In those days, Thirunavaya and Chandanakkavu were regions under the rule of the Vettathunatu Raja. Six temples were prominent in the Vettathunatu region. One of these was Thrikkandiyoor. Several great scholars proficient in various

Shrine to Mahavishnu at Chandanakkavu

Shrines to Shiva, Vishnu, Brahma, Ganapati, Saraswati at Chandanakkavu

branches of traditional knowledge lived here. Around the age of twenty, Melputhur moved to Thrikkandiyoor.

It was customary among Nambootiri brahmins for the eldest son to marry and live at the *Illam*. Younger sons did not have that privilege and travelled seeking or propagating knowledge.

Thrikkandiyoor Achyuta Pisharody was a great master of *Vyakarana, Jyotisha, Vaidya,* and *Alankara shastras.* Melputhur was attracted to Pisharody's niece. Considering that he was a well-educated young man from an illustrious family, Pisharody happily consented to their marriage. However, following his marriage, Melputhur lost all interest in learning. He began to lead an unruly life of reckless indulgence. Drowned in enjoying sense pleasures, his days had no routine or meaning. Achyuta Pisharody was deeply pained at this but said nothing.

One day, he was taking a class on *Jyotisha* seated with many disciples on the veranda of his house. It was mid-morning already. Melputhur had just woken and sheepishly made his way out to the courtyard hopping between the rows of seated disciples. Seeing this, a pained Pisharody could not help but say, "What a pity! Having acquired a noble birth as a brahmin, how thoughtlessly he squanders it away!" These words pierced Melputhur's heart. He stood there, lost, and thoughtful for a while. Then he quickly finished his bath and prayers and with all earnestness and humility prayed to Pisharody to guide him.

From then on, Melputhur was a changed person. He began to learn Panini's Grammar under Achyuta Pisharody. He studied texts on poetry and dramaturgy like *Kavya Prakasha, Alankara Sarvaswam,* and *Dasharupaka*. He also composed exquisite poetry in Sanskrit. Fully absorbed in studies, he paid no attention to anything else. Day and night he remained immersed in reading and writing. Finding in Melputhur a brilliant and worthy student, Achyuta Pisharody lavished his affection on him. Melputhur in turn revered his guru like God.

Sayanacharya in his work the *Prayaschittasudhanidhi (Sayaneeyam)* says,

पूर्वजन्मकृत्तंपापंव्याधिरूपेणजायते
तच्छान्तिरौषधौद्दनैज्जपहोमार्चनादिभिः ।

"The effect of sinful acts committed in previous births manifests as disease in this lifetime. The resultant suffering can be allayed by medicine, dana, japa, homa, archana, and the like."

Achyuta Pisharody was suddenly stricken by arthritis and became bedridden. As he was proficient in traditional medicine, he tried to treat it with medicines in consultation with other practitioners but nothing worked. The pain continued to worsen and proved too much to bear. His devoted disciple Melputhur did everything in his capacity to serve his guru and to alleviate his suffering but to no avail. Since Pisharody was a master in *Jyotisha,* he examined his horoscope. He found that the disease was the karmic consequence of sinful acts in previous births. As such it could not be cured; only endured with acceptance and surrender.

He found that acts of atonement like the performance of rituals *Tila homa, Verpadu,* and *Karmavipakadana* would relieve him of the disease and suffering. With great enthusiasm, Melputhur took the initiative to get all this done. Medicines cater only to the physical manifestation of disease in the body. The purpose of undertaking spiritual practices and ritual acts of reparation is to atone for the root karmic wrongs.

Statue of Melputhur at the Melputhur Memorial, Chandanakkavu

Statue of Melputhur inside the Guruvayur Temple

When the time came to perform the *Karmavipakadana,* Pisharody was in a quandary. It was the ritual act of transferring the effect of one's negative karma onto another individual. Only one with great spiritual power and effulgence could accept and endure the same. At this juncture everyone was afraid. Someone suggested Melputhur's name. Melputhur, who was deeply devoted to his guru, gladly came forward to be the recipient. The ritual act was duly performed and in due course, Pisharody's health improved. But soon the signs of arthritis started to manifest in Melputhur's body.

However, Melputhur was neither afraid nor upset even as the disease got worse. Different medicines and pujas were tried for the alleviation of Melputhur's suffering but none helped. A few days passed in confusion and anxiety for everyone around. Pisharody was guilty and grief-stricken but Melputhur remained unperturbed.

One day, he felt strongly that he would recover if he took refuge at the feet of Sri Krishna at Guruvayur and spent time in prayer at the temple. It was a popular belief those days that doing so cured diseases like arthritis. Many had experienced it as well. Melputhur prayed that he would go to Guruvayur as soon as he was better enough to travel. Very soon the intensity of his pain reduced. Melputhurstarted for Guruvayur with the permission and blessings of his guru and accompanied by his younger brother Matrudattan.

Thunchaththu Ezhuthachan the great poet, hailed as the father of the Malayalam language and, a contemporary of Melputhur was informed of this decision. Ezhuthachan sent a message that Melputhur should "partake of fish". Being a brahmin Melputhur did not eat fish but understood that Ezhuthachan was advising him, the advice laced with humour, to sing of Sri Krishna's glories in His ten incarnations starting with the *Matsyavatar!* Melputhur resolved that he would indeed compose a new work based on the *Srimad Bhagavata* extolling Krishna's *leelas*.

The next day, he reached Guruvayur. He planned to compose ten verses each day and thus in a hundred days to compose the work which would be a summarised version of the *Bhagavata*.

After finishing his morning bath and *sandhyavandanam* early, he prayed at the temple, offered *manasa* puja, and chanted Vedic hymns in praise of *Bhagavan* Vishnu. Circumambulating the shrine, he sat facing Guruvayurappan and composed verses. When a new verse occurred to him, he immediately recited it aloud to *Bhagavan* and Matrudattan transcribed it faithfully. At lunchtime, Melputhur would have the *naivedya*. On completion of the daily quota of ten verses, he spent the rest of the time reading the *Bhagavata*, chanting, or doing more circumambulations. This was his routine. He spent all his waking hours in the temple. At night, after the final *Athazha Puja* in the temple, he slept at some comfortable spot.

Matrudattan was ever at his brother's service diligently looking into Melputhur's needs every moment. Ten verses make one *dashaka*, and in a hundred such *dashakas*, Melputhur composed the *Narayaneeyam*, the highly venerated devotional scripture of Kerala.

The first couple of days passed uneventfully. On the third day, Melputhur's pain worsened. It seemed as though he would have to return home. Assisted by Matrudattan, Melputhur somehow managed to get to the temple but was unable to do anything thereafter. Watching other devotees effortlessly offer worship he suffered immense mental agony. The verses composed that day reflect the depth of his pain, physical as well as emotional. The third *dashaka* of the *Narayaneeyam* is thus a tug of war between the magnitude of suffering and the

Melputhur's days of intense sadhana –
composing the *Narayaneeyam*

Melputhur has Venugopalamurti's darshan

strength of devotion. Ultimately devotion won.

Apart from the first couple of *dashakas*, each one thereafter ends with the plaintive plea, "O Compassionate One! Please cure me of this disease!" Days passed thus. Melputhur battled on braving every moment of pain holding on steadfastly to his faith, firmly convinced that Guruvayurappan would cure him. Until the day he composed the ninety-ninth *dashaka*, Melputhur struggled and suffered tremendously.

Finally, the hundredth day dawned. Melputhur stood before the sanctum sanctorum. His heart was full. It was the final day of his herculean sadhana. There was nothing more he could do other than stand before *Bhagavan* in complete surrender. He shut his tear-filled eyes and prayed offering all his effort at *Bhagavan's* feet. He was not prepared for what happened next. When he opened his eyes, Melputhur beheld the resplendent form of Guruvayurappan as *"Venugopalamurti"*, the divine cowherd boy, holding His flute. While others went about offering prayers at the sanctum as usual, Melputhur beheld the Ocean of Compassion blessing him with a bewitching smile. He stood transfixed, tears streaming down his face, hairs standing on end, his entire being bathed in bliss. One-pointed sadhana and *saranagati* had awakened the inner vision through which Melputhur was able to perceive the divinity in the idol. It is this vision of Guruvayurappan that Melputhur describes in the hundredth *dashaka*, beginning with the famous verse:

अग्रेपश्यामितेजोनिबिडतर-क्लायावली-लोभनीय
पीयूषाप्लावितोऽहंतदनुतदुदरेदिव्यकैशोरवेषम् ।
तारुण्यारम्भरम्यंपरमसुखरसास्वाद-रोमाञ्चीताङ्गै-
रावीतंनारदाद्यै-र्विलसदुपनिष-त्सुन्दरीमण्डलैश्च ।।

"I see before me a bluish radiance rendered exceedingly alluring by clusters of kalaya flowers. At this sight, I feel an upsurge of bliss like one bathed in ambrosia. Next, at the core of this Brilliance, I see the form of a Divine Boy, charming in His budding youth. He is encircled by sages like Narada thrilled with ecstatic bliss and by a bevy of beauties who are the embodiments of the Upanishads."

Needless to say, with this divine vision Melputhur was completely cured of the disease. The hundredth *dashaka* is thus a top-to-toe description of the magnificent form of Guruvayurappan that Melputhur was blessed to behold. The *dashaka* ends with a prayer for a long life of good health and well-being not just for him but for all who recite or listen to the hymn.

Contemplating his life while composing the *Narayaneeyam*, Melputhur came to the realisation that the disease manifested as his only true ally; for it was pain and suffering that tore his attention away from the intellectual intoxication of scholarly gatherings and the lures of sense pleasures. It was insurmountable pain that ruthlessly drove him to meditate on Guruvayurappan and to contemplate Vedantic truths. Had it not been for suffering, he would have postponed these for some distant future and his life would have ebbed away even as he remained engaged in intellectual and other pursuits.

He expresses this thought in one of the many standalone verses composed at the time. This is reminiscent of Kunti's prayer after her sons regained the kingdom following the battle of Kurukshetra. Kunti neither questions Krishna regarding the suffering they had to undergo nor prays for a peaceful life thence. On the contrary, she beseeches Krishna for more suffering.

विपिदःसन्तुनःशश्वत्तत्रतत्रजगद्गुरो ।
भवतोदर्शनंयत्स्यादपुनर्भवदर्शनम् ।।

(Srimad Bhagavata 1.8.25)

"I wish that all those calamities would happen again and again so that we could see You again and again, for seeing You means that we will no longer see repeated births and deaths."

The fervour with which one calls out to God when in pain, whether physical or emotional, is unparalleled. Offering pain and suffering to God, washing His feet with one's tears, the devotee gets closer and closer to Him. There is only so much that the world can offer as a solution to any suffering. Ultimately, we must seek all answers within ourselves in the light of our own sadhana and devotion. Suffering can either harden and embitter us or open the doors to deeper understanding and compassion; the outcome depends on what we seek to meet with it – the world or the Divine. His guru's words had awakened Melputhur to his foolishness and turned his life to seeking knowledge. But the true import of those words and of the opportunity his noble birth afforded dawned on him only with the manifestation of arthritis in his body. It is from the depth of this realisation and total self-surrender, watered every moment by suffering, that each verse of the *Narayaneeyam* was born.

The *Narayaneeyam* is both a poem as well as a devotional hymn. Melputhur was just twenty-seven when he composed the work and was blessed with the darshan of Guruvayurappan. Various verses in the *Narayaneeyam* reveal his deep knowledge of the *Srimad Bhagavata,* various *Puranas,* Vedas, *Yogashastra, Sankhyashastra, Vyakarana,*

Vedanta, Shaiva Agama, Mantrashastra, the *Bhashyas* of Shankaracharya and the works of Madhavacharya. But it is the sentiment of unalloyed bhakti and self-surrender that renders the hymn unique and full of sweetness. Nurtured and softened by bhakti, Melputhur's *jnana* blossomed into an offering of timeless beauty and a blessing to generations of devotees.

After regaining his health, Melputhur once again became engrossed in seeking and disseminating knowledge but now Krishna-sadhana too became an intrinsic part of his life. He regularly visited Guruvayur to worship at the temple. It was during one such visit that Poonthanam approached him requesting him to read through his work and he refused. That night, stricken by arthritis once again, he had the dream in which Guruvayurappan said, "Poonthanam's bhakti is dearer to Me than your *vibhakti.*"

Even as he promptly made amends, Melputhur realised deeply that he knew and had himself written several times in the *Narayaneeyam* that *Bhagavan* bestows grace only after trampling on the devotee's ego; but the subtle ego of knowledge and spiritual attainment had reared its head in his own person. But God cares immeasurably for His devotee. Through this incident, He not only showered blessing on Poonthanam's bhakti but also saved Melputhur from ruin. In fact, Guruvayurappan's words were a testimony not only to Poonthanam's bhakti but also to Melputhur's *vibhakti.* If Poonthanam personified simple, pure devotion, Melputhur personified devotion qualified by knowledge, reminiscent of Uddhava in the *Bhagavata.*

Melputhur's knowledge continued to grow and, along with it, his fame too. Various chieftains notably, Zamorin Manavikrama, Godavarma Raja of Vatakkumkur, Veera Kerala Varma Raja of Kochi, and Raja Devanarayana of

Ambalappuzha extended him patronage. He spent many years at these palaces composing works.

His works, numbering around forty, have been classified into shastra-based or technical works, *prashastis* or panegyrics, *prabandhas* — text for *Chakyar Koothu* and *Paathakam* performances, *stotras* or hymns, and *muktakas* or standalone verses. His greatest works are in grammar — the *Prakriyasarvasvam*, the *Dhatukavyam*, and the *Apanineeyapramanasadhanam*. With the *Prakriyasarvasvam* his fame spread outside Kerala and he had correspondence with leading grammarians of the Chola country. But his most popular work continues to be the *Narayaneeyam*, adored and recited by devotees to this day.

By 1624, Achyuta Pisharody was aged and dying. His beloved disciple reached the guru's bedside and served him devotedly as he neared the end of his life. In his final moments, the guru chanted a verse beseeching *Bhagavan* Shiva, the presiding deity of Thrikkandiyoor, to whisper the *Taraka mantra* in his ear even as life flowed out of his body. Death stilled his voice before he could complete the verse but his worthy disciple did so as the guru closed his eyes, gratified.

In his own final days, Melputhur took refuge at the Mookkuthala Bhagavati temple. Known in Sanskrit as *Muktisthala*, this was also a well-known seat of scholars. In the temple surrounded by towering trees with a forest ambience, Melputhur composed the *Sri Pada Saptasati Stotra*, seventy verses in praise of the feet of the Divine Mother. In the twilight of his life, he lived serenely, engaged in worship, contemplation, and teaching. One day as he was walking towards the sub shrine after offering prayers at the main sanctum, he swooned and shut his eyes forever, peacefully, in the lap of the Divine Mother. As he had prayed in the final verse of the *Narayaneeyam*, Guruvayurappan had indeed blessed him with a long life of good health and material as well as spiritual well-being.

Today, more than four hundred years later, the Guruvayur temple is always crowded and resonant with chants. As devotees inch their way towards the sanctum through the narrow pathway, a small sign to their left says, "It was sitting at this spot that Melputhur composed the *Narayaneeyam.*" A statue of Melputhur adorns the outer circumambulatory path. The *Narayaneeyam* is recited every morning within the temple. Right outside, facing the temple is the imposing Melputhur Auditorium.

But all is quiet where once the Melputhur *Illam* stood. A statue of Melputhur stands at the site, now the property of the Guruvayur Devaswom. The family had a special relationship with *Bhagavati* at Chandanakkavu. This continues to be honoured through the practice of performing purificatory rites and worship at the spot where the family shrine used to be, before offering the ritual *pattukoora* to *Bhagavati* at the temple. Above all, Melputhur lives on through the *Narayaneeyam*, offering succour and healing to millions of devotees who consider Guruvayurappan their sole refuge.

Resources

1) Bhattapadar, M.N., *Sreemannarayaneeyam*, Guruvayur: Guruvayur Devaswom, 2017.
2) Radhakrishnan, K., *Kathakaliloode Melputhur*, Kottayam: Grand Books, 2016.
3) Bhattatiri, M.N., *Narayaneeyam: Bhagavata Condensed,* Translated by Swami Tapasyananda, Chennai: Sri Ramakrishna Math, 1976.

Chapter 3

MANAVEDAN RAJA (1585–1658)

It is around ten at night. The final *Athazha Puja* and *Sheeveli* procession at the Guruvayur temple are over. The large crowd of devotees who milled around everywhere inside the temple all day, chanting, praying, performing circumambulations, or sitting around simply enjoying the ambience, have all left. The temple premises are silent. The fragrance of oil, incense, flowers, and sandal paste lingers in the air. The world is ready to ease into rest and slumber, but within the temple, a new world now opens before a few who seek it. After a long day of giving darshan to devotees, *Bhagavan* will now come out to dance!

Krishnanattam, or Krishna's dance, is a dance drama that celebrates the life of Krishna in eight parts, performed every night within the temple. The performance takes place on the northwest side of the temple, right outside the door through which devotees exit after praying at the sanctum.

At dusk, just after the *deeparadhana*, the *keli* or percussive announcement begins as a precursor to the performance.

Following this, the artistes start getting ready. After 9 pm the central oil lamp called the *kali vilakku* is lit. The percussion instruments *thoppi maddalam* and *shuddha maddalam* and idiophone instruments *chengila* and *ilathalam* are placed before this lamp. Before the performance, all artistes, including the one who plays Krishna, touch the instruments reverentially by way of seeking blessing. The musicians and drummers pick up their respective instruments. They play the *keli.*

On cue, two stage hands hold up a multi-coloured rectangular curtain behind the lamp and in front of the musicians. Behind this curtain is the sacred space of the dance. Four female characters enter this space, touch the sacred ground, and dance the *thodayam* behind the curtain. This is to invoke the blessings of Ganapati, Vishnu, and Devi and is not meant to be watched by the audience. It is after this that Krishna's story begins.

But the story of *Krishnanattam* itself began a little less than four hundred years ago. Prince Manavedan (1585–1658) of the Zamorins' royal family of Calicut (now Kozhikode) was an ardent devotee of Sri Krishna. He was greatly influenced by Melputhur Narayana Bhattathiri and Vilwamangalam Swamiyar. We do not have information about his parents or of his childhood. In 1766 when the Mysore ruler Haider Ali captured Calicut the then Zamorin Manavikraman Raja, unable to save his land and people, set fire to the palace and committed suicide. All we know about Manavedan is that he was multi-talented and was a disciple of the well-known Sanskrit scholar Thiruvegappura Anayath Krishna Pisharody and Desamangalathu Varier. Manavedan blossomed into a poetic genius as he grew up. Only two of his works, both in Sanskrit, are extant — the *Poorvabharatha Champu* composed in 1643 and the more famous *Krishnageeti* composed in

1654. Prince Manavedan reigned as the Zamorin of Calicut from 1655–1658. This is all we know about his life. This too would probably have remained unknown and he would have disappeared into the annals of history. But destiny decided otherwise. It chose to immortalise him instead, not for any kingly exploits, but for his bhakti; for the outpouring of devotion as poetry that reverberates every night within the temple to this day - the *Krishnageeti* to which *Krishnanattam* is danced.

The sixteenth and seventeenth centuries were also a time when all over the country there was a great surge of Vaishnava religious renaissance. As Swami Vivekananda observed, a religious renaissance is always accompanied by a renaissance in arts, sciences, and literature. True to it, India witnessed the blossoming of several art forms pulsating with devotion to Krishna. Royal families, particularly of Mithila, Nepal, and Assam, took great interest in nurturing such arts. In Assam, Sankaradeva created the *Sattriya* dance-drama in the setting of the *sattras* or monastery-temples to be practiced by monks as an expression of *Krishna*-bhakti. In Navadwip in Bengal, Sri Chaitanya Mahaprabhu was the progenitor of the soul-stirring *Sankirtana* music and ecstatic dance. In Tamil Nadu, Sri Narayana Teertha composed the *Krishna Leela Tarangini* in Sanskrit, inspired by Jayadeva's *Gita Govinda*, based on the life and *leelas* of Sri Krishna. These songs are danced too, to this day. *Krishnanattam* too was among these art forms and one nurtured by the patronage of the Zamorins.

The *Krishnageeti* is an exquisite work based on the tenth and eleventh cantos of the *Bhagavata Purana*, inspired by Jayadeva's *Gita Govinda*, Melputhur's *Narayaneeyam* and *Srikrishnavilasam Mahakavyam*. Incidents from Sri Krishna's life are presented in eight parts. These are *Avataram, Kaliyamardanam, Rasakreeda, Kamsavadham,*

Swayamvaram, Banayuddham, Vividhavadham, and *Swargarohanam.*

The story is that once Manavedan was in Guruvayur along with Vilwamangalam Swamiyar. Vilwamangalam was a great *yogi* who was able to see *Bhagavan* Krishna's enchanting form. Manavedan once beseeched Vilwamangalam to help him have the darshan of Krishna as well. Swamiyar replied that he needed to seek *Bhagavan's* permission. Accordingly, the next day he informed Manavedan that *Bhagavan* had agreed and that he would be able to have His darshan playing under the *ilanji (Mimusops elengi* or *bakula)* tree. To his great delight, Manavedan was able to see little Krishna playing under the tree scooping sand into coconut shells. An overwhelmed Manavedan rushed to embrace *Bhagavan* when He disappeared saying, "But Vilwamangalam did not mention a hug!" He left behind a peacock feather from His coiffure which Manavedan rushed to pick up. He rushed into the sanctum and pledged that he would compose poetry and dedicate it to Krishna. The *ilanji* tree stood at the site where the present *Koothambalam* (temple theatre) stands, to the southeast of the sanctum. An idol of Sri Krishna was fashioned from the wood of that very tree and Manavedan began to worship Krishna in the idol. He sat before the idol and composed the *Krishnageeti* with fervent devotion. A crown was fashioned with the feather as part of it. The story is that this was used as the first ever *Krishnamudi*, or crown in *Krishnanattam.*

Krishnanattam could have developed over the centuries, to its current form, with inputs from various practitioners. It incorporates elements from the now-extinct *Ashtapadiyattam*, early earthy ritualistic forms like *Theyyattam, Thirayattam, Mudiyettu* and the like as also the nuanced Sanskrit theatre of Kerala called "*Koodiyattam*". Today *Krishnanattam* is marked by delicate choreography that blends the soft and graceful

Manavedan Raja runs to hug Balagopala under the *ilanji* tree

Tali Temple, Kozhikode

lasya and the vigorous tandava aspects of dance as also the *natyadharmi* and *lokadharmi* conventions (inadequately translated as stylised and realistic respectively). In the *Krishnageeti*, Manavedan only mentions the raga and tala to be used for each song and nothing about theatre or stagecraft. How the text came to be transformed into the performance form in which we see it today is lost to us. Though the poet called his work *Krishnageeti*, it has come to be known popularly as *Krishnanattam* in the present day as it is used for attam or dance.

Krishnanattam is marked by simplicity and restraint in all aspects. This is because its purpose and goal are never the exhibition of virtuosity but the expression and celebration of bhakti. It exists solely for bhaktas and is imbued with the spirit of devotion. The style of music in *Krishnanattam* is closely related to the *Sopana* style of rendering *tyaanis* and *ashtapadis*. This is called bhakti/*bhava sangeetham*. In the intensity of bhakti, the technicalities of music or dance become very simple. It is devotion to Krishna that is the inspiration for controlled expression and fruition of all *rasas* in *Krishnanattam*. With bhakti at its core, abhinaya is transformed into *anukeertanam*, a glorification or celebration of an idea. True anukeertanam can happen only when an artiste "ceases to be". This is nothing but the state of *saranagati* and can happen only through bhakti.

Once, during a *Rasakreeda* performance, Vilwamangalam saw Krishna dance the *rasa leela* along with the artistes. Thereafter he insisted that the performance should start only after the temple hours. This is the basis of the belief that *Bhagavan* is present during the staging of *Krishnanattam*, adding to its devotional fervour.

Krishnanattam offers the devotee an understanding and experience that is beyond meanings and technicalities. For the same reason, it is more accessible than the other dance drama traditions of Kerala. That the lyrics are in Sanskrit is no obstacle since it is the articulation of emotions, rather than word meanings that happens in *Krishnanattam*. One needs to only know what the story is and who the characters on stage are to enjoy the performance; more correctly one needs to only have a heart that feels bhakti. The *lokadharmi* convention aids this by serving to concretise devotion using real objects and actions rather than formal gestures.

An example is the poignant scene where Krishna welcomes his dear friend, the poor Sudama. It is amongst the audience that Sudama makes his appearance! He comes wearing a humble *dhoti* with *vibhuti* smeared on his chest and arms. The magnificent *Bhagavan* spontaneously runs to his dear friend and embraces him again and again with overflowing happiness and love! Seeing Krishna in their midst expressing such boundless love for a humble devotee is a scene that moves the audience to tears. Krishna washes Sudama's feet with actual water and sprinkles some on Himself with a shudder of ecstasy. He then actually eats some of the flattened rice that Sudama has got Him. These acts are powerful, unforgettable visualisations of *prema* and *sakhya* bhakti and the teaching that all offerings are precious to the Divine when given from the heart.

Every little episode from Sri Krishna's life is replete with sweetness and auspiciousness and is blissful when meditated upon. The presentation of the same within the precincts of the temple suffused in the golden glow of the oil lamp in the dead of night where each episode comes beautifully alive with colourful costumes and *touryatrika* — *geeta, vadya*, and nritta - lilting music and graceful dancing — all wrapped gently in bhakti *bhava* makes it a sublime experience for the devotee.

Natya, according to the *Natyashastra*, is a yajna or sacrifice.

Manavedan Raja runs to hug Balagopala under the *ilanji* tree

Tali Temple, Kozhikode

Koothambalam

Inside the Koothambalam

This is true not only because it incorporates elaborate worship of divinities in its preparatory practices but also because the *sangatikarana* aspect of yajna is at the heart of the practice. It is the harmonious coming together of various constituents for the good of the world.

A very important aspect of preparatory practices and rituals before the performance of natya is consecrating the performance space. In the same manner, as the space and articles of worship and the person of the worshipper are protected, consecrated, and divinised before the ritual puja, the space and the person of the performer in natya too are enjoined to undergo a similar process. The fact that *Krishnanattam* is performed in the sacred space within the temple, almost directly parallel to the sanctum, consecrated with daily temple rituals and processions renders this a natya offering perfectly in tune with the injunctions laid down in the shastra. An aura of sacredness pervades every aspect of *Krishnanattam* and there is a constant reminder of the divinity inherent in the natya offering as well as all articles that are used as part of it. The *Krishnamudi*, in particular, is considered the most sacred. Before the plays *Avataram* and *Swargarohanam*, which depict Krishna's birth and his ascension to heaven respectively, the *Krishnamudi* is placed on a banana leaf and taken to the *sopanam* of the sanctum where the priest sprinkles sanctified water on it.

It is human nature to seek and enjoy beauty in the external world. Channelling this very *vasana* towards the Divine we adorn idols with beautiful jewellery and flower garlands and offer worship using the most beautiful of articles – flowers, coloured powders, lamps, sandal paste, *mudras*, music, dance. We gather all that is most beautiful and worship the Divine with these. The mind still revels in beauty, but beauty is now in service of the fountainhead of all beauty and sweetness.

The bhakta sees beauty in each aspect of *Bhagavan* and so everything about Him appears to be full of sweetness. Thus, the *Madhurashtakam* sings that every little thing about Krishna is full of *madhurya* or sweetness:

"His lips are sweet, face is sweet
Eyes are sweet, smile sweet
Heart is sweet, music sweet
Everything about the Lord of Mathura is sweet!"

Attachment to external objects, no matter how beautiful they may seem, binds us reinforcing the idea that we are the body-mind-intellect. This ultimately only brings about pain. Krishna says in the *Bhagavad Gita:*

येहिसंस्पर्शजाभोगादु:खयोनयएवे ।
आद्यन्तवन्त:कौन्तेयनतेषुरमतेबुध: (5:22)

"The enjoyments that are born of contacts (of the senses with the external world of objects) are only generators of pain, for they have a beginning and an end. O son of Kunti, the wise do not rejoice in them."

On the other hand, attachment to beauty in the Divine serves to elevate and liberate. The Divine is *Satyam, Shivam, Sundaram* — Truth, Auspiciousness, Beauty. While adorning *Bhagavan's* image, while adoring Him through worship, while celebrating His beauty through art, the mind becomes one-pointed on Him alone. Even though the devotee may understand that God is the all-pervading Consciousness, the sweetness and beauty of the form are still bewitching and incomparable. This is at the heart of all Indian art. Classical dance in India can never be reduced to mere technique. It is a

Krishna in Krishnanattam

Memorial to Manavedan Raja

path wherein the entire body-mind of the practitioner-seeker is consumed in an act of adoration and celebration of the *Sundaram* aspect of the Divine.

All dancers in *Krishnanattam* are men. In aesthetics too the Divine alone is Purusha and every other state of being belongs to the realm of Prakriti, irrespective of gender. All Indian classical art happens in this space of Prakriti and has at its core the aspiration for oneness with Purusha. It is quite evident to spectators during the performance that the dancers are all men. At times they are visible when they are waiting for their turn to dance, drinking coffee, fanning themselves, sometimes yawning, making no great effort to hide from view. However, the humanness of these actions does not take away even a bit from the illusion of the performance. They simply dance gracefully into the sacred space when their turn arrives. It is as though the understanding that the artistes and spectators are all part of the same realm of Prakriti and aspire for a common goal through their respective roles is implicit. Bhakti is feminine in its orientation where every bhakta, irrespective of gender, is "female". This implies a state of being absorbed in love, longing, and self-surrender to the *ishta devata. Sringara/madhura* bhakti in art is the expression of this state of being whether articulated by a man or woman. In art as in spiritual striving, we come to realise that in the voyage of the soul towards the Supreme, all conceptions of the body and gender are left far behind.

Every night the artistes have a great opportunity — to step out of their limited individuality and step into the limitless, sacred space of being Krishna and other characters that are part of his story. It is an opportunity to practice the expansion of consciousness. Preparatory rituals in natya have several practices which remind the artiste to leave his individuality behind and enter the space completely emptied of the sense of I-ness. One of the most prominent qualifiers of an action as *ayajna* is the absence of doer-ship. It is a profoundly transformational practice for the artiste when approached in this manner. For, every character is a space rich with insights and knowledge about some aspect of the human or divine realm of experience. The artiste can delve deep into these spaces, being a vessel holding these various states. When this authenticity of the artiste's experience meets the bhakta's aspiration, it generates the aesthetic experience called rasa.

The bhaktas have an opportunity too, to similarly step into and experience these spaces created specifically for them. The spectator, called *sahrdaya*, is one who can identify with the subject in their heart. Meanings that resonate with their hearts give rise to *bhava* which is the origin of rasa which then pervades the body like fire does dry wood.[1] This is possible only when the *sahrdaya's* heart is pure like a spotless mirror.[2]

The experience of rasa is characterised by a state of *laya*, of *visranti*, or rest in one's own consciousness. The aesthetic state of consciousness is no longer associated with the limited "I" but with the transcendence of it, albeit temporarily. For this reason, it is referred to as *brahmaasvaada sahodara*[3] , twin of the experience of *Brahman*.

---

1 *yo'artho hṛdayasaṁvādī tasya bhāvo rasodbhavaḥ*
śarīraṁ vyāpyate tena śuṣkaṁ kāṣṭhamivāgninā (Natyasastra 7.13)

2 *nīrmalahṛdaya mukure satitanmayībhavanayogyatopeta āhita rasāsvāda sāmājikāḥ*
Abhinavagupta, **Abhinava Bharati.** quoted in N.P Unni ***Natyasastra*** Vol 1. p. 5.

3 *sattvodrekād akhaṇḍasvaprakāśānandacinmayaḥ,*
vedyāntarasparśaśunyo brahmāsvādasahodaraḥ
lokottaracamatkārapräṇaḥ kaścit pramātṛbhiḥ,
svākāravad abhinnatvenāyam āsvādyate rasaḥ
Rasa is tasted by qualified persons. It is tasted by the virtue of the emergence of satva. It is made up of full Intelligence, Beatitude, and Self-Luminosity. It is void of contact with any other knowable thing, twin brother to the tasting of Brahman. It is animated by a camatkāra of a non-ordinary

Thus, abhinaya is never meant to be merely acting, miming, or pretending; it is the act of leading the spectator to such experience.

In the *Natyashastra*, Bharatamuni says, "What final goal the scholars of Veda reach, what final goal the performers of yajna reach, what final goal the benefactors reach, that same goal is attainable by natya. The gods are not as pleased by the worship with perfumes and garlands as they are delighted by the auspicious scenes in natya."[4]

Those who watch *Krishnanattam* have probably not heard of the *Natyashastra* or how art could lead to a transcendental experience. It does not matter; for the experience is in the practice, unique and deeply personal, to each seeker whether artist or spectator. But it is experienced more effortlessly and deeper by one who seeks, longs, and aches for the Beyond in all things, including art.

And yet, today, *Krishnanattam* performance has also been envisaged as a means to fulfil desires. Accordingly, devotees can make offerings of the plays. *Avataram* and *Swayamvaram* are offered for the birth of a child and marriage respectively, *Kaliyamardanam* to offset the effect of poison, *Rasakreeda* for the well-being of unmarried girls and to end disputes between couples, *Kamsavadham* to overcome enemies, *Banayuddham* to accomplish wishes, and *Vividhavadham* for prosperity and favours related to agriculture. *Swargarohanam*, to attain a peaceful death and salvation, is rarely performed. Every year starting on the *Vijayadashami* day the eight plays are

---

nature. It is tasted as if it were our very being, in indivisibility. Visvanatha, ***Sahityadarpana***. quoted in R. Gnoli, ***The Aesthetic Experience according to Abhinava Gupta.*** p. 47.

4 *Yā gatiṛ vedaviduṣāṁ yā gatiṛyajñakāriṇāṁ*
Yā gatiṛdānaśīlānāṁ tām gatiṁ prāpnuyāt hi saḥ (Natyasastra 36–77)
Na tathā gandhamālyena devāstuṣyanti pūjitāḥ
Yathā nāṭyaprayogasthaiṛnityaṁ tuṣyanti mangalaiḥ (Natyasastra 36–79)

performed in sequence. On the ninth day, *Avataram* is repeated as it is considered inauspicious to end the story with *Bhagavan's* ascension to heaven. At other times individual plays are performed as offerings by devotees every night except from June to the end of August when the artistes rest and undergo body conditioning treatments and training. Any number of devotees can make an offering for a specific play on a particular day and the performances are booked weeks in advance.

Across the temple traditions of India, we find the propitiation of the deity through rituals as a vehicle to realise both mundane and momentous human aspirations; but it is doubtful if anywhere else an artistic rendition of the story of the deity becomes an offering to propitiate Him. The faith invested in the potency of the artistic representation of the story is an unparalleled testimony to its efficacy and edification. Despite the worldly concerns that are associated with it and are probably the preeminent motivation for offering a performance today, the possibility of the art becoming a vehicle for transcendental experience nevertheless remains.

It is for an audience of one — Sri Krishna — that the artistes perform each night. It does not matter if anyone else is present or not! They do not perform for the world's applause but for Krishna alone, bringing alive His timeless story night after night. It is a tradition that breaks all commonly held ideas and expectations of what 'performance' is. In truth it is not performance, but sadhana. The idea that Krishna comes to enact His own story is one unparalleled in the temple tradition of India. During the day, people from all walks of life, of all ages, with emotions ranging from exhilaration to anguish to despair to devotion, jostle for a fleeting darshan of Krishna in the temple sanctum. But in the silence and tranquility of night, a whole world of Krishna opens offering the bliss of

Statue of Manavedan Raja inside the Guruvayur temple

Tali Temple, Kozhikode today

immersion and serene contemplation. Night is the sacred time when yogis remain awake in meditation. *Krishnanattam* invites us to do the same, night after night. Thus, all rituals, all art, and all worship offer us a choice; with these, we may choose to seek the ever-changing world or the one changeless Truth.

It is nearly 2 am when the performance is over. The oil lamp is put out; flowers strewn on the floor are picked up. The space is cleaned and the artistes leave. Devotees gather themselves and slowly walk out of this magic world where Krishna just danced. Outside, the sky is inky black. There is barely an hour to get some sleep before the temple opens at 3 am for the *Nirmalyadarshan*. Elsewhere in the temple, preparations for the same are already underway. Krishna at Guruvayur never sleeps! His compassion keeps giving of the experience continuously. Queues for the darshan have already formed. Very few who inch past the *Koothambalam* would know that, that was where the *ilanji* tree once stood where Manavedan had little Krishna's darshan. It takes a few moments to readjust to the world outside.

Teaching Dhruva about the eight limbs of Yoga, Narada instructs him how to practice *dharana* and dhyana – by visualising and meditating on the beauty of *Bhagavan's* form, His heart-bewitching exploits, and Him as the in-dweller of all beings.[5] As he walks away, the devotee silently carries within him the joyous divine world of Krishna to be brought alive every time he shuts his eyes in contemplation.

Manavedan was sixty-eight when he composed the *Krishnageeti*. He had stayed in Guruvayur for several years before he became the Zamorin. Even afterwards he did not choose to stay in Calicut, as was customary, but shifted his administrative offices to Guruvayur. In the early days, the

5 *Srimad Bhagavata: The Book of Divine Love, p. 195–196.*

Krishnanattam performance was exclusively owned by the Zamorin family and they looked after the artistes who were under their administrative control. All gurus and artistes were based in Calicut. They travelled to Guruvayur and back once a year, where performing an entire cycle of plays in the temple was mandatory. On their way, they performed in temples, palaces, and Nambootiri households.

Manavedan died in 1658 at the age of seventy-three. His body was cremated in the palace premises at Guruvayur, south of the temple, where a lamp was kept constantly burning thereafter. For a long time afterwards, when the artistes travelled annually to Guruvayur, they concluded the performances of the season with *Banayuddham*. This was called the *pettivachukali* or the "box-closing" performance and was presented facing south, the realm of Yama so that Manavedan could witness it. This was the only time they performed facing south. This is no longer practiced.

The land reform laws introduced by the Kerala Government that came to power in 1957 rendered the Zamorin of Kozhikode financially impoverished. He was forced to dismiss the *Krishnanattam* troupe under him. The ownership of the troupe was transferred to the Guruvayur Devaswom under which it functions at present. Today *Krishnanattam* is presented at select venues outside the Guruvayur temple as well. There are two troupes so that the temple performances are never affected.

Manavedan's palace was acquired by the Guruvayur Devaswom, the structure was demolished, and a rest house was constructed. At the spot where Manavedan was cremated, his statue was erected. Manavedan offered his *Krishnageeti* to Guruvayurappan on the thirtieth day of the Malayalam month of *Tulam* (mid-October – mid-November). The Guruvayur Devaswom celebrates this day as *Krishnageeti* Day every year.

A complete reading of the text is arranged in such a way as to end on this day. A *Manaveda Suvarna Mudra* has also been instituted to encourage *Krishnanattam* artistes who are now Devaswom employees. The Zamorin of Calicut gives away the *Krishnageeti* Award for the best book of poems in three years during the famous *Revathi Pattathanam*, in addition to an award for a *Krishnanattam* artiste.

These changes may have inevitably altered some aspects of the art as it is practiced ... the link between the artistes and the art and between the artistes and the spectators. The closeness of these relationships may have suffered to some extent. But despite everything, there is still a magic bond that holds it all together. It is the unbreakable bond that devotees have with Guruvayurappan; the one Truth that remains ever changeless.

Even from the very little information that we have about Manavedan's life, it is amply evident that it was one sanctified by love and longing for Krishna. *Bhagavan's* vanishing before Manavedan could hug Him or have his wish of the darshan fulfilled was a gift of grace. For, it must have left His devotee at the peak of his longing. Without intense longing, it is impossible to know God. This longing would only have further intensified thereafter, leading him to worship the ilanji idol and pour his heart into verse. It is that very longing that continues to be celebrated through *Krishnanattam* and stoked in the hearts of devotees as they watch it; in the woman who once offered to suckle the small child who played baby Krishna, in the old woman that prostrated and offered *dakshina* — money and flowers — at the feet of the little boy who played the child Krishna, in the devotee that quietly wipes away a tear watching Krishna appear, every time, with a scattering of flowers.

After all, there is no difference between Krishna's name, His form, and His story. Intertwined in every aspect of the cultural life of India, from music to painting, from sculpture to scripture, from poetry to dance, it is Krishna's story that keeps alive the unfading beauty of His name and form in a million ways. Rich imagery and richer tapestry weave the strands of His story in the hearts and minds of devotees. Manavedan immortalised Krishna's story in Guruvayur. His enduring memorial is no statue, but this; immortalising not just his memory but also his love for Krishna. His enduring legacy is also this; not just an art form called *Krishnanattam*, but art as sadhana, as a medium of longing and love.

THE TALI TEMPLE COMPLEX

The Tali temple complex is a significant spot connected to the Zamorins. The Zamorin traditionally visited the Tali temple following his coronation. The Zamorin's palace was adjacent to the north-western part of the temple.

The Tali temple complex, the fourteenth century water tank of Mananchira, and the Mishkal Mosque in Kuttichira are the only remnants we have of the Zamorin period in addition to the *Kovilakams* (palaces) of Mankavu and Thiruvannur being the palaces that survived.

Recently, the District Tourism Promotion Council (DTPC) and the local MLA fund jointly worked on a restoration project at the Tali temple pond complex. The pond is now bordered by restored bathing ghats, pavilions, and a wide walkway with relief murals that depict scenes from the Zamorin period like the Zamorin's coronation, royal procession, the Mamangam trade fair, the Revathi Pattathanam, *Krishnanattam*, Thyagaraja music festival held near the Tali temple, and Mangattachan.

THE REVATHI PATTATHANAM

An annual assembly of scholars which was traditionally held under the Zamorin's patronage. It was a major event in South India in the medieval period. A seven-day competition among Vedic scholars, it was and continues to be one of the highlights at Tali. Eminent scholars of the past like Uddanda Shastri of Tamil Nadu had participated in the contest in the past. The Revathi Pattathanam is held during the Malayalam month of Tulam (mid-October to mid-November) every year.

Resources

1) Seth, P., *Heaven on Earth: The Universe of Kerala's Guruvayur Temple,* New Delhi: Niyogi Books, 2009.
2) Elayad, P.C.V, *Krishnanattam (Krishnageeti),* Guruvayur: Guruvayur Devaswom, 1986.
3) Unni, N.P., *Natyasastra,* Delhi: Nag Publishers, 1998.
4) Bharucha, R. "Preparing for Krishna", *Theatre and the World: Performance and the Politics of Culture,* London: Routledge, 1993.
5) Panikkar, K.N., *Sopanatatvam: The Tradition and Philosophy of Sopana Music,* Translated from Malayalam by Sulini V. Nair. Bhopal: Amaryllis, 2016.
6) Sukumaran, K. in *Bhaktapriya,* Guruvayur: Guruvayur Devaswom, September 2012.
7) Gnoli, R., *The Aesthetic Experience According to Abhinava Gupta,* Varanasi: Chowkhamba Sanskrit Series Office, 1985.

Chapter 4

VILWAMANGALAM SWAMIYAR (1575-1660)

Villumangalam Swamiyar, known popularly as "Vilwamangalam Swamiyar" is a prominent name in the spiritual and cultural tradition of Kerala and many parts of India. Even as this is so, much of his life remains shrouded in mystery. Due to the popularity of his devotional masterpiece, the *Sri Krishna Karnamritam,* he became a legendary figure, and several parts of India like Bengal, Orissa (now Odisha), and Andhra claimed him as their own. However, there are scattered historical references to the fact that he was born in Kerala, and some scholars hold that there have been at least five personages who were known as Vilwamangalam Swamiyar. This is because stories connected to this name lie dispersed across centuries. Three of them are definitely known from various periods in time.

It is also not impossibility that these could well have been one person! Such spiritual mahatmas, who had astounding mastery over the laws of the physical world and who transcended these with ease, were not uncommon in ancient

India. Kerala too had such personages, even in very recent history, who lived much longer than the average human life span. It is impossible to understand such phenomena with the logic we use to understand the everyday world. When the ranges of even our visual and auditory capacities are laughably limited to a few wavelengths and frequencies, how do we even begin to grasp the range and depth of subtle phenomena and realms unfathomable by our gross faculties?

Vilwamangalam was a yogi who could see deities with his physical eyes. Many temples have such stories to tell. The origin of several temples across Kerala in places like Thiruvananthapuram, Thiruvarppu, Ettumanoor, and Cherthala are also linked with Vilwamangalam Swamiyar. Anecdotes linking him with various well-known historical figures who lived during different periods are also aplenty.

What we know regarding the antecedents of the yogi/s is presented here. The birthplace of the first Vilwamangalam is believed to have been a place called "Sukapuram". He is said to have lived in the eighth century.

The great poet Ulloor S Parameswara Iyer in his seminal work *Kerala Sahitya Charitram* mentions that there has been only one personage by the name Vilwamangalam and that he lived in the thirteenth century at a place called Puthenchira, a village in the Mukundapuram taluk of Trichur (now Thrissur) district. He is referring to the second Vilwamangalam who, according to one research, lived between 1575–1660.

The dates are confusing; nonetheless, the second Vilwamangalam is considered a contemporary of the great devotees Poonthanam, Melputhur, Manavedan Raja, and Kururamma. He was a great personality not just of Guruvayur but also of his era. An unknown yogi blessed Vilwamangalam with a *mantra* and he sought the boon of seeing little Krishna at least once a day. As mentioned earlier, he was closely associated with several temples in Kerala like Cherthala Karthyayani, Thiruvarppu, Ambalappuzha, and of course Guruvayur.

The first canto of his *Sri Krishna Karnamritam* hints that his father's name was Damodaran and his mother's was Neeli. From the words "*leelasukena rachitam*" (composed by Leelasukan) in a verse, some scholars deduce that his name was Leelasukan. There are also claims that his name was Akshayan and that he was a disciple of Patanjali Maharishi. Yet another claim is that his name was Krishnan and that he took *sannyasa deeksha* from the Thekke Matham, Trichur. Vilwamangalam states that his guru belonged to the Thekke Matham, believed to have been founded by Padmapadacharya, a direct disciple of Adi Sankaracharya.

Sanskrit works mention him as belonging to the house called *Kodandamangala* or *Chaapamangala*, Sanskritised forms of Villumangalam. *Kodanda* or *chaapa* mean bow. *Villu* in Malayalam and Tamil also means the same. The name must have changed to Vilwamangala or Bilvamangala when it moved to other parts of India. Other regions not being well-versed with the word *villu* would have assumed it to be *bilva* or *vilva*, (*Aegle marmelos*, or wood apple) whose leaves are considered holy and used for the worship of *Bhagavan* Shiva. Some commentators of the *Karnamrita* have also made-up stories about a *vilva* tree in front of his house, from which he derived his name!

No definitive records are available about his early life. There are only stories relating to how he took up *sannyasa*. One widely recounted story is about Vilwamangalam falling in love with the beautiful and accomplished Chintamani who was also a great devotee herself. While practicing austerities at the Vatakkumnatha Shiva temple in Trichur as per his father's instructions, the young Vilwamangalam happened to see Chintamani in the temple premises. No longer able to concentrate his mind, he managed to find her house and expressed his desire to marry her. She asked him to return in eight days. He was so smitten that he braved several hardships in the dark, stormy, new moon night to reach her abode. Chintamani was aghast to see him at her doorstep in such inclement weather.

However, Chintamani was also aware of a divine aura around Vilwamangalam. Orphaned as a child, she was deeply devoted to *Bhagavan* Shiva. After their marriage, Vilwamangalam found it impossible to stay away from her. Having gone to perform the rites of obsequies for his father, he had returned home without performing them, unable to bear the pain of separation from his wife. Saddened by his inordinate attachment to her, even at the cost of his duties, Chintamani took him to the shrine room and advised him not to waste his precious human birth in such mad pursuit of sense pleasures. She advised him to direct his attachment towards God instead and that if he did so, even liberation would become easy.

These words fell upon Vilwamangalam's heart like a shower of grace and completely transformed his mind. He bowed before Chintamani and from that moment on, considered her as his guru. Then and there, he sat down and lost himself in meditation before the sacred *Salagrama*. Soon he had a vision of *Bhagavan* Krishna as *Balagopala*. Overwhelmed, Vilwamangalam fell at His feet. The vision disappeared but the bliss that filled Vilwamangalam's heart began to flow as poetic verses soaked in bhakti. Chintamani quickly wrote them down on palm leaves.

He started the very first verse with the words *Chintamani jayati* paying tribute to her.

Vilwamangalam and Chintamani –
composing the *Sri Krishna Karnamritam*

Vilwamangalam sees Guruvayurappan in the hearts of all

चिन्तामनिर्जयतिसोमगिरीर्गुरुर्मे
शिक्षागुरुश्चभगवान्शिखिपिञ्छमौलिः
यत्पादकल्पतरूपल्लवशेखरेषु
लीलास्वयंवररसम्लभतेजयश्रीः

"My guru Somagiri, who is like the chintamani — the wish-giving stone — to me, is victorious. Sri Krishna, who wears the peacock feather in His hair, is victorious as the guru who instructs. To those who wear on their head the Lord's feet, which are like the sprouts of the wish-fulfilling Kalpaka tree, Vijayalakshmi – the Goddess of Success - comes of her own accord; as the bride in search of a suitable bridegroom garlands him at her svayamvara."

By daybreak, the *Sri Krishna Karnamritam* had been composed!

Vilwamangalam realised that Chintamani was no ordinary woman. Chintamani too understood that her husband's life had a larger purpose. It was a new dawn in their lives. Chintamani accompanied him to the riverbank. As he stepped into the boat, he mentally prostrated before her greatness and bid farewell to her and to the life he had lived thus far.

Some distance into the river, the boat shook wildly and blood-stained water bubbled onto the surface where the boatman had dug his pole. Vilwamangalam jumped into the water, concerned that some creature was hurt. But instead of a creature, he found a beautiful idol of *Bhagavan* Krishna, the exact form he had seen in the vision, bleeding at the chest where the pole had pierced. As he held the idol, Vilwamangalam felt divine power enter his body. He heard a celestial voice say, "Hold Me close to your heart and meditate on Me. From now on we will journey together!"

Disembarking, he wandered here and there, for a long time,

as an *avadhuta*. Finally, he returned to his native village. He found a suitable place close to his ancestral home – a barren piece of land with boulders. A temple was built there and he consecrated the idol therein. The temple came to be called: "*Paramel Thrikkovil Sri Krishna Kshetram*" — "the Srikrishna temple upon boulders".

With Krishna's name constantly on his lips and form in his heart, Vilwamangalam worshipped *Balagopala*. Little Krishna regarded Vilwamangalam as His father and constantly played pranks around him. Once, Vilwamangalam scolded *Balagopala* for defiling the puja articles and pushed him away. He disappeared saying Vilwamangalam would need to go to *Ananthan Kaadu* (Forest of Anantha) to see Him again.

Heartbroken, Vilwamangalam left the place in search of *Ananthan Kaadu*. Visiting many temples along the way, he wandered distraught in search of his beloved *Balagopala*. Finally, one day he overheard a woman scold her child for misbehaviour, threatening to throw him into *Ananthan Kaadu*. Overjoyed, Vilwamangalam set off according to the directions she gave him. In the thick forest, he had the darshan of *Bhagavan* Vishnu in the *Ananthasayanam* pose along with Devi Mahalakshmi. He prostrated before *Bhagavan* and found his *Balagopala* before him once again asking for something to eat! Vilwamangalam quickly begged for some grains of rice and fire and cooked it in a coconut shell. Crushing some tender mangoes along with it, he offered naivedya to *Balagopala*.

Vilwamangalam did not beseech *Balagopala* to return with him to his native village, for he too had left it when *Balagopala* disappeared. Little Krishna promised Vilwamangalam that whenever he wished to see Him, He would be there. And thus, Vilwamangalam set out once again wandering from place to place, temple to temple, for the rest of his life.

Hearing of the divine presence of *Bhagavan* Vishnu in

Ananthan Kaadu the Maharaja of Travancore constructed a temple, the Sree Padmanabhaswamy temple, and consecrated the idol of *Bhagavan* as "*Ananthapadmanabha*". The Maharaja also built a Swamiyar Matham for Vilwamangalam to stay, close to the temple and he regularly performed *pushpanjali* at the temple. Going by the historicity of the Sree Padmanabhaswamy temple, this story perhaps must be attributed to the first Vilwamangalam. We may not claim anything with certainty because stories seem all intertwined! However, it is the essence of bhakti at the core of these stories that we need to savour.

As regards the stories of Vilwamangalam and Guruvayur temple, once during a *Rasakreeda* performance of *Krishnanattam*, which was at first conducted on the eastern side of the temple, Vilwamangalam noticed that the idol in the shrine was just a lifeless statue. When he looked towards where the performance was taking place, he saw two Krishnas dance the *mullappoochuttal* sequence, in which Krishna deftly weaves his way in between the gopis. It is believed that he advised the authorities to change the performance area to the northern side and to delay the starting time to ten at night when the sanctum would be closed.

It was only in 1947, after a long struggle, that the Guruvayur temple was opened to Hindus of all castes. Before this, there was only one occasion when everyone could enter and worship at the temple. This was during the Guruvayur *Ekadashi.* The Guruvayur *Ekadashi* which falls on the eleventh day of the bright, waxing fortnight of the Malayalam month of *Vrischikam* (mid-November to mid-December) is considered especially sacred. This is so for three reasons. It is believed to have been the *Ekadashi*, the day before the Kurukshetra war, when Krishna imparted the *Bhagavad Gita* to Arjuna and through him, to all of mankind. It is also the

Paramel Thrikkovil Srikrishnaswamy Temple

Statue of Vilwamangalam inside the Guruvayur temple

anniversary of the day when Sri Sankaracharya laid down the details of the pujas and rituals to be followed at the Guruvayur temple. It is also the day when Melputhur had the darshan of Guruvayurappan.

For three days — the *Dashami* day before *Ekadashi*, the *Ekadashi* day, and the *Dwadashi* day afterwards — the temple would be open to all. It was a very extraordinary event at a time when caste restrictions were stringently enforced. A well-known story is that Vilwamangalam felt extremely uneasy surrounded by massive crowds of lower caste devotees during Ekadashi and complained to Guruvayurappan. There is also a version that it was another brahmin who felt this way, who complained to Vilwamangalam. *Bhagavan* is said to have asked Vilwamangalam to look closely at the devotees. To his utter surprise, he saw in the person of each devotee, Vishnu's cosmic form with four arms. He realised deeply that *Bhagavan* indeed dwelt in all and no one was inferior or superior.

There is a small room on the northern side of the quadrangle called the *Nrittam Muri* or the dance room. It is said that Vilwamangalam used to dance here in ecstasy after seeing Guruvayurappan.

Thus, Vilwamangalam spent his days going from one temple to another, each of which became a divine site for many wondrous stories and miracles. Around the twilight of his life, news reached him about an aged sannyasini, a devotee of *Bhagavan* Krishna, whom everyone called "*Dasiamma*". She went about visiting various temples and rendered the *Sri Krishna Karnamritam* melodiously. She also guided devotees advising them based on divine insight. She was also an eloquent speaker and prolific writer, composing devotional poetry and literature. Hearing of her greatness, Vilwamangalam desired to meet her.

Once he was invited to a temple, where Dasiamma too was

staying at the time, during the event of a major puja. Hearing that the great Vilwamangalam would arrive, Dasiamma made all necessary preparations. While staying at this temple, a little boy from the neighbourhood called "*Unnikuttan*" grew very attached to Dasiamma. Whenever she thought of him, he would be near her ready to help with anything.

When Vilwamangalam arrived at the temple, Dasiamma was ready to welcome him with all ritual formalities. He could not believe his eyes seeing the face that glowed in the light of the oil lamp. It was none other than Chintamani! He had not imagined in his wildest dreams that Dasiamma known for her melodious rendering of the *Sri Krishna Karnamritam* was his beloved Chintamani he had given up decades ago. Her hair had greyed and body had wrinkled with age. But her face shone with great effulgence. Tears of joy flowed from Chintamani's eyes as she recognised her husband.

As she welcomed him and showed him to a seat, Unnikuttan came running. He stood there smiling at Vilwamangalam with twinkling eyes. Vilwamangalam immediately recognised the little Krishna he had scolded long, long ago for defiling his puja articles! Both he and Chintamani had aged, but the divine child had remained the same! He prostrated at Unnikuttan's feet as Chintamani looked on, bewildered. As they both felt immensely blessed, *Balagopala's* form faded away.

That night, Vilwamangalam had a vision in which *Bhagavan* told him that it was time for both of them to leave the physical plane and that Thalakkulathoor Bhattathiri would guide them. The very next day, they set out to meet the Bhattathiri who had divined of it all. Legend has it that he instructed them to follow two sannyasis, who were divine beings, and they guided them to *Vaikuntha*.

The stories may seem beyond possible, but the gem of bhakti that is wrapped and hidden securely within these cannot be missed.

Apart from the *Sri Krishna Karnamritam*, Vilwamangalam is said to have composed around twenty more works including the *Kalavadham Kavyam, Kalashtakam, Dakshinamurtistavam, Ramachandrashtakam, Sreechihnam,* and *Purushakaram*. These works reveal his sound scholarship in several branches of learning — not only technical knowledge related to grammar or language but also of *apara vidya*.

However, *Sri Krishna Karnamritam* was his magnum opus, through which he came to be widely known. In this work, his pure love for *Bhagavan* finds profound and delicate expression through his exquisite poetic skills. In three cantos with more than 300 verses in all, it is an emotional outpouring of devotion with the verses arranged in no clear order. While in certain verses the devotee pines for *Bhagavan*, some others are suffused with the joy of divine realisation. The sweetness of the verses is not only in the meaning of their content but also in the way they sound — truly *karna-amrita* or ambrosia for the ears! The predominant emotion is *premabhakti* or divine love and the devotee who listens to it too, enjoys the blessing of being filled with nectarine divine love.

It is believed that during his visit to southern India, Sri Chaitanya Mahaprabhu found the first canto of the *Sri Krishna Karnamritam* from Kerala and took it to Bengal. It then became a code of religious worship for the Vaishnavites. From Bengal itself, we have around nine interpretations of this work.

The Paramel Thrikkovil Sri Krishnaswamy temple has a specially designated space where Vilwamangalam Swamiyar has been consecrated. This is the only temple in Kerala where Vilwamangalam Swamiyar is thus consecrated and worshipped. This is probably the very first temple in Kerala to *Balagopala* as well.

The Travancore State, Paravur taluk, Puthenchira village, Revenue Settlement Register Survey of 1885 mentions a plot belonging to Sri Vilwamangalathu Nambootiri. People around the area encroached upon this land and eventually became owners, getting their ownership ratified by the Village Office. Eventually, only four to five cents of rocky land around the Anappara region were left. There is a cave beneath this place which is supposed to have been a Jain cave temple. This area is believed to have the presence of Vilwamangalam Swamiyar and continues to have rituals conducted. There was also a belief that heartfelt prayers with areca nut and betel leaf offerings at Anappara would undoubtedly yield results.

Anappara is situated some distance south of the Paramel Thrikkovil Sri Krishnaswamy temple. This was where Vilwamangalam Swamiyar is said to have been born. This historically significant place was also home to the Kurur *Illam* where the great devotee Kururamma is said to have lived and the Chemmangat *Mana* of another staunch devotee Chemmangat Nambootiri.

There is also a claim that Vilwamangalam's house is the same as Vella *Illam* of Tavanur (*Tapanoor* - the *tapasvi's* land). The courtyard and what is left of the basement of this *Illam* still exist. *Yogeeswara* Puja continues to be performed on Vilwamangalam's death anniversary at the Vella *Illam* basement, in the belief that he is here.

It is believed that the Thirunavaya Navamukunda Temple close by was built for Swamiyar's mother to offer prayers to *Bhagavan* Vishnu in her old age. In the Guruvayur Sri Krishna temple, Vilwamangalam's statue adorns the outer circumambulatory path, along with other great devotees.

Though a great *jnani*, Vilwamangalam's devotion blessed him with countless darshans of *Bhagavan* and an intimate relationship with Him. As he sings in a verse, if one has pure devotion for *Bhagavan*, liberation and other values of life will do him voluntary servitude!

करारविन्देनपादारविंदम्
मुखारविन्देविनिवेशयन्तम्
वटस्यपत्रस्यपुटेशयानं
बालम्मुकंम्मनसास्मरामि । (Canto 2, verse 57)

"I meditate on the infant Mukunda who sleeps on the leaf of a banyan tree with his lotus-like foot placed in his lotus-like mouth with his lotus-like hand."

Resources

1) Seth, P., *Heaven on Earth: The Universe of Kerala's Guruvayur Temple,* New Delhi: Niyogi Books, 2009.
2) Prof. K.P Narayana, *Sri Krishna Karnamrutham*, Pisharoti, Guruvayur: Guruvayur Devaswom, 2015.
3) Pottaykkal, R., *Sri Vilwamangalam Swamiyar,* Trichur: Krishnanjali Publications, 2013.
4) Sreekrishna Sarma E.R., "Vilvamangala" in *The Vedanta Kesari,* Vol. 46, Issue 1, 1959.

Chapter 5

KURURAMMA (1570–1640)

Kururamma's very life was an exquisite song of Guruvayurappan's praise! Born Gauri, she belonged to the Purayannur *Mana* in Palakkad, Kerala. Even from a young age, she was very deeply devoted to *Balagopala*.

At just eleven, she was married into the Kurur family, also originally from Palakkad, but later settled in the Vengilassery village in Thrissur. At Kurur Illam, she had her own shrine room with all the necessary facilities to worship Krishna.

One day, a sannyasi came to the *Illam* and requested for food. Among the various food items, he was also served a little bit of the *naivedya* offered to *Bhagavan* that morning. It was exceedingly tasty. But it may not have been just the taste that prompted the sannyasi to enquire who had prepared and offered the naivedya. The little girl was brought before him. Seeing her sparkling eyes and divine face, he asked her to sit before him and initiated her with a mantra. He advised her to chant it constantly, with devotion, and that she would then be blessed with the darshan of Sri Krishna. Hearing this, she forgot herself and asked, "Will I be able to see *Bhagavan* at all times?" The sannyasi smiled, "Most certainly. Pray with single-pointed love. Your wish will certainly be fulfilled." She obeyed implicitly and soon was blessed with Krishna's darshan. This little girl later came to be known as "Kururamma".

The Kurur *Illam* was in a dilapidated condition and the poor family struggled to live. But they did not deviate the least bit from the dharmic path. Despite such adherence to *dharma*, fate was not kind. Kururamma's husband suddenly died one day, leaving her all alone. In those days, Nambootiri widows lived very difficult lives of strict seclusion, constant fasts, and vigils. Not made part of any happy occasion, they were shut off from the world and all joys. The young, vibrant child – now a widow – found herself facing an unhappy future. In great sorrow, she turned to her beloved Krishna for succour. Like Poonthanam, she too gradually transcended her sorrow considering Guruvayurappan as her child.

She spent her days and nights in the thought of Guruvayurappan alone. Whatever food she had, she first offered Him and only then partook of it. Gradually her life settled into a routine. She knew nothing about the happenings in the world outside. Her days were spent in prayer, chanting, and worship. But after some time, she felt a kind of dissatisfaction. She yearned for the living presence of *Balagopala* as her constant companion; someone she could see, hear, love, and share her sorrows with. As the days went by, her prayers and austerities grew more and more intense. Her need for food and sleep dwindled. Her entire being was concentrated on one thought — Guruvayurappan.

Days turned into months and years and the child widow Kururamma grew into adulthood and old age; her whole life had been one unbroken contemplation on her *Balagopala*. Her limitless *vatsalya* bhakti freed her soul from the sorrows of her mundane existence. It now soared constantly in a world of endless bliss.

One hot summer day, Kururamma was sitting inside the house as usual, absorbed in *japa*. A man's weary voice was heard outside, asking for water to drink. Kururamma felt tormented, for being a Nambootiri widow, she could not step out to give water to a stranger. As she sat there helpless, a small boy rushed inside, took a pot of water, and rushed out. The stranger very gratefully drank all of it, thanked the boy, and went his way. The boy placed the water pot back in its place and ran away. Kururamma was stunned. Before she could gather herself, he had gone! She rushed outside looking for him, but he had vanished. From that day, he became a regular at Kururamma's *Illam*, her enthusiastic, constant helper in all her work.

Whenever Kururamma enquired about his antecedents, he deftly evaded the topic. All she knew was that his name was Narayanan and he was called "Unni". Her heart swelled with motherly love for the child. He picked flowers, washed and arranged the vessels for worship, chopped vegetables for her, and was with her all the time. She, in turn, lavished affection on him.

One day, an old Nambootiri arrived at Kururamma's door, writhing in pain. She had just concluded her worship. She offered him the *naivedya* prasad and lunch. He told her it had been years since he had eaten a full meal due to his constant stomach pain. There was no treatment he had not tried. He had even approached Vilwamangalam, to learn that his suffering was his *prarabdha* that had to be endured. Tears flowed from the man's eyes. Kururamma said, "Take my word, chant *Achyutananda Govinda Madhava* constantly and you will be well." She also assured him that she would pray for him. Upon her insistence, he ate his fill and left. Soon he found that his pain had indeed vanished.

Statue of Kururamma inside the Guruvayur Temple

One day, Kururamma came to know that the great Vilwamangalam was at Trichur, only six miles from her village. She was excited because she knew he was a great soul who experienced *Balagopala's* real presence every day during his puja. She desired to invite him home for *bhiksha*. Without worrying about the propriety of a poor widow like her inviting the great Vilwamangalam home, she sent her invitation through a servant. When Vilwamangalam accepted it, she was overjoyed. She explained to little Unni how they had to make every effort to get ready in two days, for Vilwamangalam was no ordinary devotee. He was someone before whom Guruvayurappan came and sat in person to accept his puja! Unni did not seem to think much of it, for he felt *Balagopala* was constantly with Kururamma too. Kururamma scolded the little boy for his absurd observation and got busy with preparations. Unni too got busy arranging flowers and washing and cleaning the premises.

On the day of the *bhiksha*, Kururamma was surprised to meet the lady of the wealthy Chemmangat *Mana* at the temple tank, already having finished her bath and in a great hurry. She usually came much later. Since Kururamma too was in a hurry, she took her customary three dips at the far end of the tank. Chemmangat Amma got annoyed with Kururamma for 'defiling' her by splashing water on her inadvertently. Kururamma was shocked and hurt, also to learn that Vilwamangalam would be at the *mana* for *bhiksha* that day. Crushed and heartbroken, she returned to the *Illam*, heavy with grief. She sobbed piteously as Unni hugged and consoled her, wiping away her tears. He assured her Vilwamangalam would surely arrive. Somehow his words gave Kururamma confidence and they continued the preparations.

Vilwamangalam and the eldest at Chemmangat *Mana* had been childhood friends, so he had readily accepted the invitation to *bhiksha* that had come the previous evening. In his excitement about meeting his friend, he forgot all about Kururamma's invitation. Among other arrangements, a conch had to be blown when he started. But no matter how hard they tried, no sound came from the conch that day. A shocked Vilwamangalam understood there had been some mistake on his part. A moment's introspection and stung with remorse, he jumped up and shouted, "Our *bhiksha* today is at Kurur, not at Chemmangat!" All conches gave out glorious sounds at this.

At Kurur, Vilwamangalam was stunned to find the flowers he offered *Balagopala* during *archana*, fall at Unni's feet. But he did not reveal this to Kururamma as per *Bhagavan's* wish. As he took leave after *bhiksha*, he most respectfully remarked how blessed she was that *Bhagavan* Vishnu was doing her constant service and sought forgiveness for having caused her sorrow. A perplexed Kururamma replied she was but a poor woman who did not deserve such praise at all.

After a while, Kururamma began noticing that soon after she had offered *naivedya* to *Balagopala*, the vessels would all be empty. She suspected Unni but since he was so helpful, she did not feel like asking him. But one day, she caught him red-handed. She boxed his ears, brought him out of the puja room, 'imprisoned' him in a huge pot, black with soot, and sat down right next to it. For some time, he cried begging to be freed, but gradually grew silent. Kururamma imagined that he might have slept off. When she checked, she was stunned to find the child was not in it!

Meanwhile, Vilwamangalam was most disturbed to find that *Balagopala* had not manifested during his puja that evening. He felt tormented wondering if his ego was the reason for *Bhagavan* keeping away from him. Waiting and waiting for *Balagopala* to come, Vilwamangalam drowned in anguish.

Suddenly, he beheld *Balagopala* come running, looking all upset, His beautiful body and face all grubby, covered entirely in soot! Cobwebs hung from His earlobes and His hair was without His favourite peacock feather! Vilwamangalam was shocked. Panting, *Balagopala* said that despite His begging to Kururamma that His father was waiting for Him, she had not freed Him; she had punished Him for eating the payasam that was rightfully His! Vilwamangalam took Him on his lap and gently cleaned the soot off Him as his eyes filled with tears and heart swelled with wonder and devotion at *Bhagavan's* sweetness and mercy.

Every day Kururamma offered a gooseberry to *Balagopala* who loves tender mangoes and gooseberries. She kept a year's supply of gooseberries with her. One day, she found a large number of gooseberries fallen from the tree in the courtyard and gathered them. She put them on the verandah and went to get a vessel. By the time she returned, she found half of them gone! She suspected Unni and looked around, but then, a sweet voice spoke from inside. Kururamma turned to see Unni's angelic face. He said, "It was Krishna who stole the gooseberries, Mother, please do not scold Him!" Kururamma's eyes filled with tears. From that day she never missed her gooseberry offering.

Unknown to her, Kururamma spent every moment in the living presence of *Balagopala* in the form of Unni. Her consciousness was fully absorbed in Krishna. She fed Him, played with Him, spoke to Him, and loved Him with all her being as He remained constantly with her, doing all her chores for her. Until the end of her life, Kururamma did not know that the little child who waited upon her all day, helping her and playing naughty pranks, was none other than her beloved Bhagavan who had fulfilled her childhood prayer of wanting to see Him all the time.

Kururamma's naughty little Unni

Kururamma Srikrishna Temple

All her life, she had constantly sung,

कोमलम्कूजयन्वेनुम्श्यामलोऽयंकुमारकः
वेदवेद्यम्परम्ब्रह्मभासतांपुरतोममः ।

"May this beautiful, dark child, who is in truth Brahman Himself, be pleased to grant me darshan, playing on His flute!"

And her prayer had been answered even before she had known it.

It is said that like Poonthanam, *Balagopala* led Kururamma also to *Vaikuntha* in her mortal coil. But Kururamma still lives in the minds of Guruvayurappan's devotees as the epitome of *vatsalya* bhakti and mother to *Bhagavan* himself. The outer circumambulatory path in the Guruvayur temple also has Kururamma's statue along with that of the other devotee saints.

As time went on, most of the property of Kurur *Illam* was sold or encroached upon except for a small bit of land in Vengilassery village, which lay unoccupied for about 350 years. In 2002, an *Ashtamangala Devaprasna* revealed the strong presence of Sri Krishna in the form of *Balagopala*, connected with a woman, at a particular place in Vengilassery. On further probing it came to light that it was Kururamma with *Balagopala*. A temple to Balagopala, the Kururamma Sri Krishna Temple, was constructed there with a memorial for Kururamma.

Resources

1) Seth, P., *Heaven on Earth: The Universe of Kerala's Guruvayur Temple,* New Delhi: Niyogi Books, 2009.
2) Pravrajika Ajayaprana, "Koororamma" in *The Vedanta Kesari,* May -August 1981.
3) Pottaykkal, R., *Sree Vilwamangalam Swamiyar,* Trichur: Krishnanjali Publications, 2013.

EPILOGUE

THE GLORY OF THE DIVINE NAME

Is it possible to have darshan of God as these stories tell us?

Once, Swami Yatiswarananda asked the same question to Swami Brahmananda, his guru, and among the foremost disciples of the great mystic Sri Ramakrishna of Bengal. He believed that the visions of baby Krishna that the lady devotee Gopaler Ma had, belonged to the transcendental plane. "How can one see God in the external world with physical eyes?" he had asked. Swami Brahmananda replied simply, "Show me the line of demarcation where matter ends and spirit begins." Swami Yatiswarananda understood these words to mean that when the eye of the spirit opens, one sees Brahman everywhere.

When we study his works, we come to realise that Poonthanam was no simple, ignorant devotee. On the surface of it, he was an ordinary man with no great education, who struggled to make ends meet. Wrongly judging him thus initially, even Melputhur had not accorded him much respect. But Poonthanam was a living example of the truth that a devotee who constantly chants the divine name would come to manifest true devotion and wisdom, all within himself.

He presented deep Vedantic philosophy in the simplest Malayalam in his *Jnanappana*. Other works like the *Santhanagopalam Pana, Sri Krishna Karnamritam,* and *Nootettu Hari* too are testimony to his deep knowledge. Thus, we see that after exploring the various paths to the Divine, he had finally chosen the one that was the easiest and most beneficial to humanity – the path of *nama sankeertana* bhakti, i.e., of devoted chanting of the divine name. Through his life he showed us that an individual would be able to grasp the essence of all shastras and attain knowledge, dispassion as well as the highest state, all through chanting the divine name.

Melputhur was a highly venerated scholar well-versed in several shastras. But through his life, we see that there are limits to the distance that scholarship can take us in our journey to the Divine. Manavedan Raja was an erudite royal. Vilwamangalam was a yogi and sannyasi. Kururamma was but a poor widow who spent all her life within the confines of her house, doing household chores.

These five great devotees of Guruvayurappan together represent a cross-section of humanity; people from different walks of life engaged in very different pursuits. The only thing they had in common was bhakti, their immense love for Krishna. It does not matter where one is born, or what one's station in life is. Bhakti is only about the heart, how one loves God, and how one loses oneself in such *prema*. When pure devotion dawns within, the devotee begins his inner voyage to the Beloved. All else that is required is added to him automatically. All of them had plunged into the very depths of their souls, constantly yearning for Krishna. And they were all blessed to see *Bhagavan* Sri Krishna with their physical eyes.

In each of these stories, we see how it was never any kind of attainment that brought *Bhagavan* to the bhakta – it was only pure love of the purified heart. It was solely through the awakened power of the divine name that each of these great devotees had experienced Krishna.

The shastras advise that *japa* is the easiest way to grow spiritually in *Kali Yuga*. Constant japa makes the mind calm, steady, one-pointed, and purified and it finally loses itself in the *ishta devata*. *Japa* along with meditation upon the chosen deity brings fast results. But it must not be superficial. One must lose oneself day and night in contemplation. All these devotees are examples of such intense sadhana and unceasing practice. Without unceasing practice, there can be no spiritual experience.

A word produces within us its associated idea and an idea, when deepened, produces the sense of its reality. This is the philosophical basis of *japa*, as well as its beauty. Repetition of the divine name clarifies the Divine Consciousness more and more until it eventually becomes vivid. It is said that if one does nothing but practise *japa*, spending hours at it, the mind becomes purified and calm, and the senses lose their appetites.

Chaitanya says,

"Such is the effect of the repetition of the name of God, it purifies the mirror of your heart, so that God becomes reflected in it, and this terrible fire of worldly existence, which has engulfed us, becomes extinguished. It emanates the light of goodness all around and knowledge comes alive through the

repetition of the name.

And the ocean of joy begins to heave high. From time to time, you begin to have upsurges of spiritual joy within. At every step, you find more and more joy comes, and then you feel as if you have been bathed in the ocean of nectar. Victory be to such repetition of the name of God!"

Chaitanya, "Eight Slokas of Instruction", verse 1.

Philosophical knowledge alone will always remain just dry knowledge. The knowledge of God comes alive through the repetition of the name.

Chaitanya also describes the spirit in which japa needs to be practised.

तृणादपिसुनीचेनतरोरपिसहिष्णुना
अमानिनामानदेनकीर्तनीयसदाहरिः

"Humbler than a blade of grass, more patient than a tree, without conceit pride or egotism, chant constantly, the name Hari."

When established thus in japa, one reaches the beginning of the higher kind of devotion – raganuga bhakti – the path of pure love, wherein one finds it impossible to live without loving God and tasting His love and joy. Such a person begins to find the details of the external world hazy and in its place feels the loving divine presence.

हरेरनामैवनामैवनामैवममजीवनम् ।
कलौनास्त्येवनास्त्येवनास्त्येवगतिरन्यथा ।।

"Hari's name alone, name alone, name alone is my life; in

Kali (yuga), there is no other way, no other way, no other way, than this." (Naradiya Mahapurana 41:115)

Resources

1) Swami Ashokananda, *Ascent to Spiritual Illumination,* Mayavati: Advaita Ashrama, 2007, p. 196.
2) Swami Yatiswarananda and Swami Prabhavananda, *The Eternal Companion: Life and Teachings of Swami Brahmananda,* Madras: Sri Ramakrishna Math, 2016, p. 6.

GLOSSARY

Annaprashan – a baby's ceremonial first feeding of rice.

Ananthasayanam – *Bhagavan* Mahavishnu as reclining on the serpent Anantha.

Apara vidya – knowledge obtained through the intellect and the senses comprising all empirical and objective knowledge.

Archana – worship with flowers.

Ashtamangala Devaprasna – a practice of the prasna branch of Hindu astrology which uses eight (*ashta*) auspicious (*mangala*) objects. *Ashtamangala Prasna* is used to find the unknown causes of undesirable situations in people's lives and to plan remedial actions. When applied in the context of the life of Hindu places of worship, it is called *Ashtamangala Devaprasna*.

Ashtapadi – songs from the *Gitagovinda.*

Athazha Puja – the final puja of the day.

Avadhuta – an ascetic who has renounced all worldly attachments and connections.

Balagopala – Little Krishna.

Bhagavan – God

Bhagavati – Goddess

Bhakta - devotee

Bhakti – devotion

Bhava – feeling; emotion.

Bhiksha – alms; a meal.

Brahman – Supreme Consciousness.

Dana – charity

Darshan – sight of a divine being.

Deeparadhana – worship with lamps.

Dharana – Keeping the mind collected, holding the breath suspended, steady abstraction of the mind, followed by placing *Bhagavan's* image in the mind to the exclusion of everything else. One of the rules of *Ashtanga* Yoga.

Dhoti – a garment consisting of a piece of material tied around the waist and extending to cover most of the legs.

Dhyana – meditation, contemplation.

Geeta – music

Gopis – cowherd girls.

Hari nama – the divine name of Hari.

Homa – fire sacrifice.

Illam – the ancestral home of the Nambootiri caste.

Ishta devata – chosen deity.

Japa – chanting

Jnana – knowledge

Jnani – man of knowledge.

Madhura bhakti – the devotional attitude of seeing God as one's beloved.

Mahatma – great soul.

Mahima sthali – a place of spiritual significance and glory.

Mana – the ancestral home of the Nambootiri caste.

Manasa puja – mental worship.

Mantra – sacred formula.

Matsyavatar – the first of Mahavishnu's ten incarnations in which He took the form of a fish to save primeval man from the deluge that consumed the earth.

Mullappoochuttal - one of the most famous dance compositions in Krishnanattam, performed on two occasions – as part of the Avataram story and Rasakreeda.

Naivedya – consecrated food offering

Natya – performance with dance and emoting.

Nirmalyadarshan – the very first darshan of Guruvayurappan at 3 am.

Nritta – dance

Pavithra (ring) – traditional ring with an intricate knot design.

Payasam – sweet pudding.

Prakriti – Cosmic Nature.

Prarabdha – destiny; experiencing the fruits of actions performed in previous births.

Prasad – consecrated offering.

Prema – divine love.

Puja – ritual worship.

Purusha – Cosmic Being.

Pushpanjali – worship with flowers.

Raga – melodic modes used in Indian Classical music, a series of five or more musical notes upon which a melody is made.

Rasa – aesthetic experience.

Rasa leela – Krishna's dance with the gopis.

Roga – disease

Sadguro – O venerated teacher!

Sadhana – spiritual practice.

Sakhya bhakti – the devotional attitude of seeing God as one's friend.

Salagrama – a fossilised ammonite considered to represent Sri Mahavishnu.

Sandhyavandanam – a mandatory ritual act traditionally supposed to be performed by Brahmins three times a day.

Sangeetham – music

Sannyasa deeksha – initiation into monkhood.

Saranagati – complete self-surrender.

Shastra – scripture

Sheeveli – the procession of the deity at the temple premises in the morning and late evening. It is a procession of caparisoned elephants, one of them carrying the idol of *Bhagavan*.

Sopanam – steps

Sringara – love

Swargarohana – ascent to heaven.

Tala – rhythm

Taluk – an administrative division and an entity of local government.

Tapasvi – ascetic

Taraka mantra – a powerful mantra believed to have the power to liberate the soul from the cycle of birth and death.

Tyaani – a hymn in couplet structure.

Upadesha – advice

Upadevata – minor deity.

Upanayanam – a ceremony where a Brahmin boy wears the sacred thread for the first time. An upper caste ritual of initiation of a male child's life as a student (brahmachari) and his acceptance as a full member of his religious community.

Vadya – instrumental music.

Vaidya – a practitioner of traditional medicine.

Vairagya – dispassion.

Vasana – mental tendency.

Vatsalya bhakti – the devotional attitude of seeing God as one's child.

Vedadhyayana – learning of the Vedas.

Vibhakti - In Sanskrit, *Vibhakti* is a system of grammatical case endings that are used to indicate the syntactic function of nouns, pronouns, and adjectives in a sentence.

Vibhuti – sacred ash.

Vishnu Sahasranama – the thousand names of Sri Mahavishnu.

Yogi – great spiritual personage.

ACKNOWLEDGEMENTS

This book would not have happened if not for the following people and I am deeply grateful to each of them.

My father told me I should write about Poonthanam and the Poonthanam Illam when we first visited there. I didn't take it very seriously, but when I later spoke about that wonderful visit to my friend Dr. Vikram Sampath, he told me there was no way this should remain unwritten. That is how the idea of writing about the five devotees came about, particularly because there was no such book in English available.

Renowned author and speaker, Sri. N. Somasekharan shared books, thoughts, and valuable insights which helped immensely while writing. My heartfelt gratitude to him. The articles were first published as a series in the Vedanta Kesari magazine of the Sri Ramakrishna Math. Deep gratitude to the then editor of the magazine, Swami Mahamedhananda for his constant encouragement and support in working on the book.

Ms. Pepita Seth's magnum opus on Guruvayur – *Heaven on Earth: The Universe of Kerala's Guruvayur Temple* – is an exhaustive and inspiring work, just like all her other books. It was my great good fortune that she agreed to write a Foreword for this book. My deep gratitude to her for readily agreeing to do this at a time when she was preoccupied with many matters! Many thanks to Ms. Kaneez Zehra Razavi, editor of my first published translation, and since then a dear friend, and Sri Ganesh Vancheeswaran, who have been great sources of guidance.

Thanks to my dearest friend Anjali Menon who I would turn to for advice or opinion on every little thing to be met only with readiness and generosity, every time. Artist Sri Sajeev Sebastian has drawn beautiful sketches of evocative moments from each article. The cover too has his drawing. My gratitude to him. Gratitude also to Sri Surendran of Saritha Studio, Guruvayur, for helping me with photographs for the book.

I thank my family for their silent, supportive presence in my life and everything I do; especially my father for his constant concern and interest in all my activities, and my little Amrit, who makes me wonder every moment how Krishna's mischief must have been!

My deepest gratitude and prostrations to my guru – Amma – Mata Amritanandamayi, and to Guruvayurappan for making all of this happen.

ABOUT THE AUTHOR

Sulini V. Nair is a Mohiniyattam practitioner and writer. Having received advanced training in Mohiniyattam under *Padma Shri* Bharati Shivaji, she has worked extensively in dance researching, teaching, writing, and performing at some of India's noted classical dance festivals. She was awarded the National Scholarship to Young Artistes from the Ministry of Culture, Government of India for advanced training in Mohiniyattam. Her interest in exploring dance as a body-mind practice further led her to train in Laban Movement Analysis and Bartenieff Fundamentals. She has collaborated with artists across genres, presenting innovative works in India and Australia and presenting lecture demonstrations and papers. She is the founder-director of Svatva, a centre for women to work with movement, dance, healing, and self-empowerment. She has also worked in television and radio scripting and presenting programmes on environment, culture, and spirituality.

Sulini has contributed articles on art, culture, and spirituality to various magazines. Working with the legendary theatre director Kavalam Narayana Panikkar, she translated his seminal work *Sopanatatvam* into English. A few other translations are in various stages of publication.

She is a post-graduate and rank holder in Economics from the University of Calicut with a postgraduate diploma in English Journalism from the Indian Institute of Mass Communication, New Delhi. She also has a Distinction Certificate in Anatomy and Physiology from the Imperial Society of Teachers of Dancing, London. She was nominated to the Senate of the University of Calicut for her contribution to art and culture.

She also works part-time as an independent ecosystem professional with a Mumbai-based knowledge company.

Contact: snair.dance@gmail.com

ABOUT INDUS SOURCE BOOKS

Indus Source Books is a niche, independent book publisher in Mumbai passionately committed to publishing good and relevant literature. We believe that books are one of the most important mediums of communication and we seek to bring out publications that help to serve the community and the world we live in.

At Indus Source Books, we celebrate the diverse spiritual traditions, culture, and history of the world and present it to our readers in a contemporary format that retains its essential flavour: "Indian Spirit, Universal Wisdom."

Use the QR code below to visit our website.

Indus Source Books
42/43C, Balaji Bhavan,
Sakal Bhavan Road, Sector 11,
CBD Belapur, Navi Mumbai 400614
INDIA
www.indussource.com | info@indussource.com